Life
IN A BUCKET OF SOIL

Life
IN A BUCKET OF SOIL

Alvin Silverstein
and
Virginia Silverstein

Illustrated by
Elsie Wrigley

DOVER PUBLICATIONS, INC.
Mineola, New York

To the memory of our parents,

Edward and Fannie Silverstein
and
Samuel and Gertrude Opshelor

Bibliographical Note

This Dover edition, first published in 2000, is an unabridged republication of
the text and illustrations from the work originally published in 1972 by William
Morrow and Company, Inc., New York. In the 1972 edition, the pseudonym
"Richard Rhine" was used by the authors.

Library of Congress Cataloging-in-Publication Data

Silverstein, Alvin.
     Life in a bucket of soil / Alvin Silverstein and Virginia Silverstein ; illus-
trated by Elsie Wrigley.
          p. cm.
     Originally published: New York : William Morrow and Co., 1972.
     Includes bibliographical references (p.   ), index.
     Summary: Describes the various animals that live within the soil under our
feet, including earthworms, roundworms, snails, mites, beetles, and ants.
     ISBN-13: 978-0-486-41057-9 (pbk.)
     ISBN-10: 0-486-41057-9 (pbk.)
     1. Soil animals—Juvenile literature. [1. Soil animals.] I. Silverstein,
Virginia B. II. Wrigley, Elsie, ill. III. Title.

QL110 .S56 2000
591.75'7—dc21
                                                                          00-026400

Manufactured in the United States by Courier Corporation
41057905
www.doverpublications.com

Contents

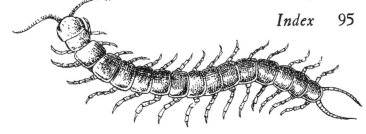

The world of the soil.

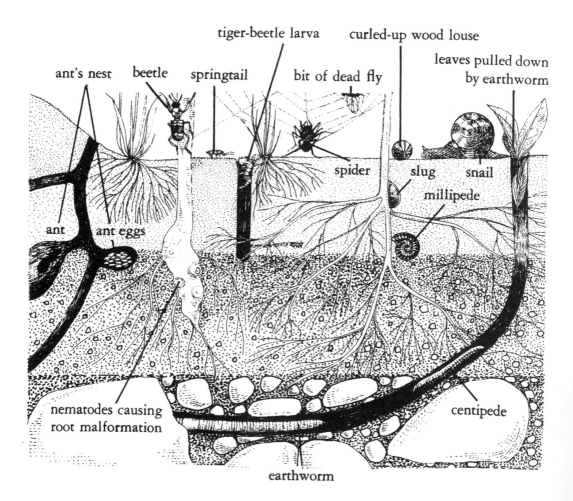

World in the Soil

THERE IS A WORLD OF LIFE BENEATH OUR FEET. THE SOIL OF every meadow, forest, and field swarms with tiny creatures. Even in the city, vacant lots and strips of dirt along the sidewalks have their own life forms.

In these worlds below, countless numbers of animals are born, struggle for life, and die.

The realm of the soil is like a vast underground jungle. Branching roots of plants twist and twine in all directions. The strangest creatures scurry and slither along these rootways. Some have giant jaws that can snap an enemy in two in a single crunch. Others bristle from head to toe. Many are completely blind, yet they know where they are going at all times. They would have no use for eyes, for they never leave the darkness of the soil.

The world within the soil is shaken now and then by rumbling avalanches. Earthworms are churning their way through the soil. The tunnels they leave behind them help to bring fresh air into the underground cities. Indeed these earthworms are the great "builders" of the hidden realm. Their burrows become the housing projects for countless numbers of creatures. No sooner are the burrows made than beetles and other many-legged animals invade them, seeking shelter. They venture up to the world above, snatch up some insect eggs or other morsels, and scoot back to their new-found homes. Other insects find their prey within the soil tunnel. Here fierce battles may be fought, and the price of defeat is to be the meal of the victor.

The soil is a vast restaurant filled with the strangest delicacies—old decaying roots and rotting leaves, the bodies of dead, half-devoured insects, bits of animal droppings that beetles and other soil dwellers have brought underground. These may not seem very appetizing to us, but to many creatures of the soil they are nourishing foods. Earthworms, beetles, and many tinier inhabitants of the soil break down the bodies of dead animals and plants and return the chemicals they contain to the soil. This helps to provide fresh nutrients for the growing plants. Delicate root hairs, so small they cannot be seen without a strong magnifying glass, take in moisture and chemicals from the surrounding soil. They in turn send out chemicals of their own, which change the lives of the creatures that inhabit the underground realm. Some of these plant chemicals are powerful pesticides, far more potent than any that humans have been able to make. Other chemicals act like signals that keep the roots of nearby plants from growing too close.

The lives of the tiny citizens of the world of the soil are linked together in many complicated ways. Some feed upon the decaying matter of the soil. These creatures, in turn, fall prey to aggressive predators that attack and devour them. But all must die, even these predators themselves. And their dead bodies form the food for still other creatures of the soil.

This world beneath our feet seems to be cut off from our own. But this is not at all true. A farmer plowing in a field turns the world of the soil upside down and exposes countless numbers of the creatures of the dark to the air and sun, where they quickly die. Many deep dwellers are now near the surface, where the soil soon becomes dry. Many of those that do not move down fast enough are doomed to death. But the plants that grow from the seeds that are sown provide food and shelter for a multitude of creatures. A heavy rain or many days of drought can also upset the delicate balance in the soil.

Even a single footstep on the soil will change millions of lives. Delicate tunnels will collapse and air pockets will shrink. Plants will be crushed and die, and hordes of creatures living about their roots will perish. Millions more will be born and thrive upon the dead plants as they decay.

Our actions can affect the world of the soil, often without our even realizing it. The lives of soil creatures can have an equally great effect on our world of air and sunlight. Plants that grow in the soil help to provide us with our two most

Each soil layer has its own community of soil dwellers.

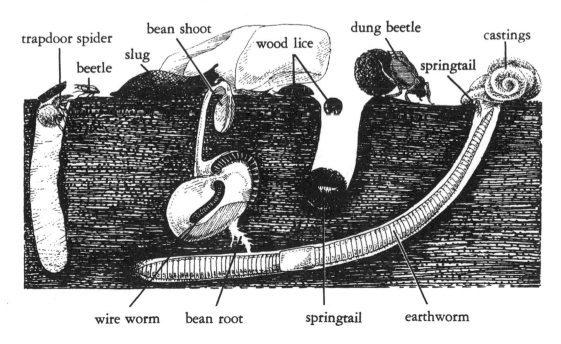

trapdoor spider
bean shoot
wood lice
dung beetle
castings
beetle
slug
springtail

wire worm   bean root   springtail   earthworm

important needs for life. Plants give us food. Everything we eat is either part of a plant, or part of an animal that ate plants, or perhaps an animal that ate other animals that ate plants. Plants give us oxygen to breathe. They produce this gas by chemical reactions inside their leaves. Scientists believe that nearly all the oxygen in our atmosphere was produced by living plants. If all the plants were to vanish from our world, our supply of oxygen would eventually be used up unless we found other ways to replace it.

Some plants live in the waters of oceans, lakes, and ponds. But nearly all of our food plants, and many of the plants that send oxygen into the atmosphere live in soil. Plants do not need to eat as we do, but they have their own necessities for life. They must have water, which their roots take in from the soil. They need some minerals, too, to build into their own special chemicals. Plants cannot use these minerals unless they are in just the right form. Four-fifths of the atmosphere is made up of the gas nitrogen. But although plants need nitrogen, they cannot use the gas from the air. There is plenty of nitrogen in the body of a dead mouse, but a plant cannot use that kind of nitrogen either — it is locked away in complicated organic chemicals. Some bacteria in the soil can take nitrogen gas from the air and build it into simple salts that plants can use. Other soil bacteria can break down the organic chemicals from the bodies of dead plants and animals and turn them into the simple salts that plants need. These bacteria are helped in their work by the actions of beetles and worms and other small soil dwellers, who feed on dead things and break them down into smaller pieces that the bacteria can get to more easily.

The activity of small soil animals and microscopic bacteria turns the remains of dead plants and animals into a substance called humus. This is a very complicated material. It contains fibers from plant leaves and stems and bits of organic matter that will break down very slowly. Humus gives soil its dark brown color and helps to bind together grains of sand and fine bits of clay to produce a crumbly texture.

Nearly all the humus is found mixed with bits of crushed rock in the top layer of soil. This topsoil may be only an inch or two thick, or it may extend down for a foot or so. The soil beneath it is made up of larger and larger stones and rocks, with very little organic matter. The roots of plants spread out mainly in the topsoil layer, drawing in the droplets of moisture trapped in the crumbly texture and taking in nourishing minerals dissolved in the soil water. Soils where a wide variety of animal life flourishes are rich in humus and useful minerals. Soils whose animal population is sparse are often stony and barren, and most plants cannot thrive in them.

The creatures that inhabit the soil range from bacteria so small that thousands could fit on the point of a pin up to furry mammals like mice and moles and woodchucks. In this book we will concentrate mainly on the "middle-sized" animals of the soil, from the size of a grain of sand up to the size of an earthworm. You would not need a good microscope to see these animals, as you would for the soil bacteria and one-celled, animal-like protozoa. But a hand lens or magnifying glass might help you to spot many interesting details that are too small for your own eyes to see.

The animal life to be found in a particular sample of soil may be quite different from that of another, even a sample taken from a different corner of the same garden. The amount of moisture in the soil, the amount of acid and other special chemicals, the types of plants growing in it—all these conditions help to determine the species of animals that can live and flourish in it. But the same basic groups of animals are found in nearly all soils throughout the temperate zones of the world —whether in England or China, Argentina or the middle of the United States. The animals you will meet in this book are those you are most likely to find in a bucketful of soil that you might dig up in your own backyard or in a nearby park or field or woods.

There is a whole new world out there under your feet, just waiting to be explored.

Safari in the Soil

HOW MANY ANIMALS DO YOU THINK YOU MIGHT FIND IN A bucketful of soil? A dozen? A hundred?

You have probably seen some soil animals while you were out on walks or digging in the garden—a beetle scurrying away when a stone was turned over, an earthworm tugged out of its burrow by a robin, an armor-backed pill bug that curled up into a ball when you touched it. Perhaps you have tried to grow plants in a pot and then dug them up to find a cluster of tiny white worms clinging to their roots. There is life in the soil, to be sure. But can you believe that a single bucketful of earth may contain *millions* of animals? And that does not even count the tiny one-celled creatures too small to be seen without a good microscope.

You can see some of these soil dwellers by sprinkling a handful of freshly scooped-up soil on a sheet of paper and quickly looking at the surface with a hand lens. For a moment the soil swarms with life, tiny pale creatures groping about in a flurry of legs and feelers. Soon they slip into cracks in the lumps of soil and vanish, fleeing the light and dryness of our world. You can scoop up larger creatures, such as beetles or earthworms, in a small paper cup. (You could use your fingers, but it might be a better idea to avoid this until you know more about your captives. They might sting or bite.) You can catch some of

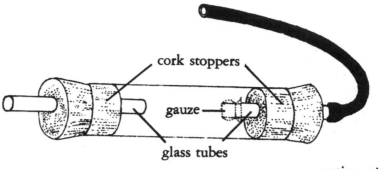

cork stoppers

gauze

glass tubes

suction pipe

the smaller creatures with a suction pipe of the kind shown on this page. But before you have had a chance to trap more than a few, the great multitude of soil dwellers you glimpsed will be gone.

Other soil animals can be caught by gently shaking a sample of soil through a kitchen sieve onto a sheet of paper. Small creatures will slip through the mesh of the sieve and fall on the paper. They will probably be startled at first and remain quite still. But then they may try to run away, and as soon as they move you will be able to spot them more easily. You can pick them up gently with a camels' hair brush or a pair of tweezers, or even a fingertip moistened with saliva. If you use a sheet of white paper, you will be able to see dark-bodied soil dwellers quite readily but may miss many pale animals that live in the deeper parts of the soil. The whitish soil dwellers show up well on a sheet of dark-colored paper.

Naturalists who study the soil have invented a number of devices for trapping small soil animals so that they can be identified and studied. Some of the apparatus they use, like the suction pipe, is simple enough to make yourself.

Many insects and other small soil animals are caught in a

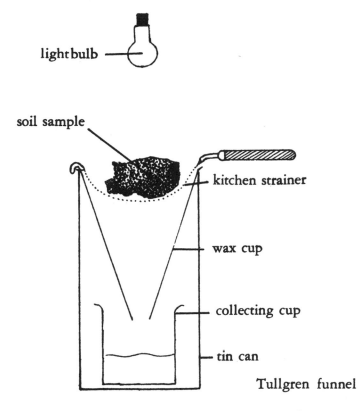

light bulb

soil sample

kitchen strainer

wax cup

collecting cup

tin can

Tullgren funnel

setup called a Tullgren funnel. A simple design is shown on this page. A sample of soil is placed in a sieve set in a cone-shaped waxed cup with a hole cut out of the bottom. Under the cone is a small cup with damp blotting paper on the bottom (if you want to try to keep the animals alive), or filled with water or alcohol (if you just want to identify and count the different kinds). Heat from the lightbulb hanging above the funnel dries out the soil. The top part, closest to the bulb, dries out first. Most of the small creatures that live in the soil live in the films of moisture around the soil particles. If it becomes too dry for them, they will die. As the soil dries out, all the animals that are able move down into the parts of the soil that are still moist. Finally they reach the bottom, slip through the sieve, and fall down the funnel into the collecting cup.

When you are using a Tullgren funnel, it is best not to break up the sample of soil, for then you risk injuring the animals that live in it, or trapping them in "islands" of soil that quickly dry out. Instead, you should carefully take out a whole lump of soil and place it gently upside down on the sieve. Then the animals near the surface of the soil can come out easily. (If the soil sample were right-side up, they would have to burrow through the whole layer of soil, and many surface dwellers are not able to burrow.) You must also be careful not to place the lightbulb too close to the soil, for if the soil dries out too rapidly, many animals will not have enough time to escape and will die. If you are going to collect living animals, you must be sure to take them out of the collecting cup quickly, before they have a chance to eat one another!

Roundworms cannot be collected in a Tullgren funnel, for when the soil dries up they usually do not move. Instead they go into a sort of resting state and wait for a rain to wet the soil again. A special kind of funnel, shown below, is used for them. This funnel is called a Baermann funnel. In the simplest form, two cone-shaped waxed cups, one inside the other (the outer one has the tip cut off) are set in the rim of a tin can.

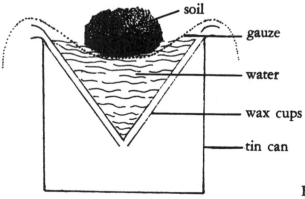

Baermann funnel

18

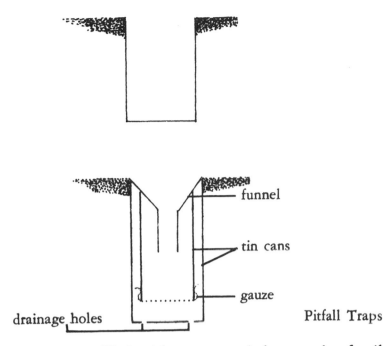

funnel

tin cans

gauze

drainage holes   Pitfall Traps

The inner funnel is filled with water, and the sample of soil is placed in a net of gauze, which hangs into the water. The roundworms are attracted into the water. Then, since their bodies are heavier than water, they sink to the bottom of the cone. After a few days, the bottom of the cone is pierced with a pin, and the water from the bottom is allowed to flow into a collecting cup. This water contains most of the roundworms.

Some animals, such as beetles and centipedes, are very active on the soil surface, but there may not happen to be any at all in a bucket of soil you dig up. You can catch some of these soil animals by setting up a pitfall trap. As you can see from the drawing above, this can be a very simple device. A tin can or jar is sunk into the soil with its rim just level with the soil surface. Insects and other small creatures running about on the surface of the soil fall in and cannot climb out because

19

the sides of the can are too smooth. You can make a more complicated pitfall trap, if you wish, with a funnel to protect your catch from birds, and drainage holes on the bottom in case it rains. You may want to fill the bottom of the trap with alcohol to kill the animals before they have a chance to eat one another.

When you collect your soil samples, you will want to take them from as many different kinds of environments as possible: an open field, a garden, a forest, or from the strips of earth along city streets; shady and sunny spots; from under rocks and fallen logs and heaps of old leaves; from dry spots and the banks of streams; and from different depths in the ground. Each kind of soil will have its own special creatures, and the same creatures will be much more numerous in some soils than in others.

One of the most interesting ways to study soil animals is to enclose soil in a box with glass sides. The box is kept in the dark except when you are looking at it. (If you use a red light, the animals may think it is still dark, for many animals are blind to the color red.) Through the glass sides you can see the creatures of the soil living together—hunting and feeding, mating and raising their young. With a hand lens or microscope you can watch the smaller creatures in action, and if you are a camera bug, you can even take pictures of them.

If you want to raise small insects or other soil creatures individually, you can make a special set of cages, like those shown on page 21. Pour about a half inch of plaster of Paris into a box, and just before it sets completely, press a row of microscope slides into the surface. After the plaster has set, remove the slides and hollow out rows of wells about half an inch deep and half an inch wide. In each of these wells you can place a bit of soil and the creature you want to raise. The rows of wells

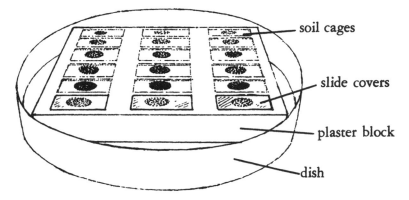

soil cages

slide covers

plaster block

dish

Soil Cages

are covered with the microscope slides to form the cages. You can keep the soil watered evenly without disturbing the soil creatures by placing the block of plaster of Paris in a dish or bowl and keeping it watered.

You can conduct a number of interesting experiments with soil animals. You can see whether they move toward light or away from it. By placing a water-soaked wad of cotton in a box or jar with a soil animal, you can determine whether it moves toward or away from regions of greater moisture. You can try various kinds of food and determine what each kind of animal likes to eat best. Once you have found out what will attract an animal, you can even set up some "intelligence tests" for it, to see whether it can learn to solve simple problems.

For example, suppose you have discovered that an earthworm normally seeks darkness and avoids the light. You can build a small Y-shaped box with a hole at the end of one arm of the Y. Shine a flashlight into the hole and place the earthworm at the entrance at the bottom of the Y. When the worm reaches the fork, it will normally crawl into the dark arm of

21

the Y. But what will happen if you place a bit of food in the lighted arm? The earthworm may crawl over to get it. If you keep rewarding it each time it crawls into the lighted arm, it may learn to disobey its natural instincts and seek the light even if there is no food waiting for it.

In experiments such as these, scientists have learned much about the habits, needs, and abilities of animals. But large parts of the world of the soil and the animals that live in it have scarcely been explored. In a bucket of soil you dig up in your own neighborhood you may discover strange creatures that have never been described before, or observe some unusual practice that has never been witnessed by anyone else.

Earthworms

TUNNEL BUILDERS

MOST PEOPLE KNOW CHARLES DARWIN WAS THE MAN WHO worked out the theory of evolution, which explained how the many forms of life developed on our planet. But few know that Darwin was fascinated by earthworms and studied them for many years. Toward the end of his life he had a favorite experiment that he showed people who visited him. On top of his piano was a row of flowerpots. Each one was filled with earth and contained one earthworm. At night the earthworms came up to the surface to get some leaves. While his pet worms were crawling about on top of the soil, Darwin would play some notes on the piano. When he played high notes, nothing happened. But when he played certain low notes, all the worms would immediately vanish into their burrows.

This amusing demonstration illustrated a number of facts about the lives of earthworms. The common earthworm, the kind that Darwin was working with, lives in a U-shaped tunnel in the soil. At night it comes up to the surface to gather leaves and twigs, which it pulls down into its burrow. It uses part of this vegetable matter to line its burrow and plug up the entrance. But part of it is a food supply. The worm moistens the leaves and other plant matter with a liquid from its body. This liquid contains chemicals that help to soften and digest the food. Later, the earthworm will tear or suck off

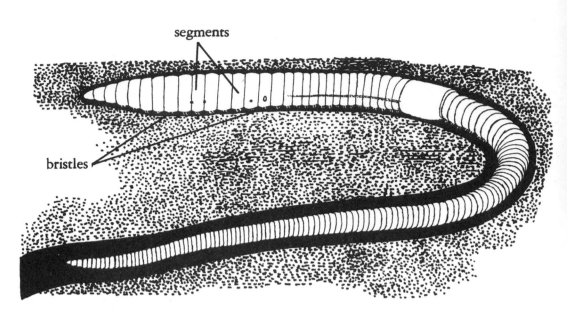

segments

bristles

The earthworm eats a tunnel through the soil, leaving castings and enriching the soil.

pieces and swallow them. Some other kinds of earthworms do not come up to the surface to feed at all. They live on the bits of plant matter already in the soil.

There is a very good reason why the common earthworm comes out of its burrow only at night. This animal is very sensitive to the ultraviolet rays of sunlight. If it is caught outside during the day, it soon becomes paralyzed and cannot move. This means death for the unlucky earthworm, for the air dries its skin. An earthworm breathes through its thin, soft skin, and it cannot do this unless it is covered with a film of moisture.

In the soil, where the earthworm burrows, there is usually plenty of moisture. Tiny cracks and channels trap and hold droplets of rainwater long after the rain. Even in a time of drought, the earthworm and other soil creatures can usually find enough moisture deeper down. But although the earthworm must have a great deal of moisture in order to live, too much water is not good for it either. When a heavy rain sends a flood of water down an earthworm's burrow, the worm will drown if it does not get out in time. Flooding is a terrible problem in an earthworm's life in two ways. If it manages to escape drowning by crawling out onto the surface, it may be caught out in the sun's rays and die. Even when there are rain clouds in the sky, enough ultraviolet rays may come through to hurt an earthworm.

Why did Darwin's earthworms flee when he played low notes on the piano? Earthworms, like most other soil dwellers, have a keen sense of touch and are very sensitive to vibrations. Darwin's pets could "feel" the piano music. This sense of touch is very useful to the earthworms in the world of darkness in which they live. An earthworm would not be able to see an enemy in its burrow, where the sunlight cannot reach. Indeed, earthworms do not even have eyes (although they can tell the difference between light and darkness when they are outside, by "seeing" with their skin). In its dark tunnels the earthworm senses the approach of an enemy by the vibrations it makes as it creeps, glides, or scurries through the soil.

The earthworm may lack a sense of sight and it cannot hear the way we do, but it does have other senses that are quite keen. It seems to be able to respond to chemicals and changes in temperature. The earthworm can taste its foods, and it can tell the difference between various kinds of leaves. Even an earthworm has favorite foods, and if you offer it several kinds of leaves, it will eat the one it likes best.

An earthworm's body is shaped like a long, slim tube, and it does not have any legs at all. It moves through the soil in an unusual way. If the soil is loose, the earthworm can dig a burrow by simply shoving pieces of soil to the sides. But in hard soil it actually eats its way along, swallowing soil at its mouth end and eventually pushing it out again at the tail end. As the soil travels through the worm's body, bits of food matter are digested, and various chemicals are added. The particles of soil that leave the earthworm's body, called castings, are thus slightly different from the soil it took in.

An earthworm moves along in its burrow by stretching out the front part of its body so that it becomes long and thin. If it tried to pull the rest of its body up while it was in that position, it would just slip backward, as it has no legs to anchor it. The worm swells up the front part of its body so that it becomes quite fat. Now it is wedged snugly in the tunnel and it can pull the rest of its body after it. Special bristles that stick out from the earthworm's body help to anchor it in the tunnel. It can pull these bristles in when it wants to slide smoothly through the soil. The earthworm can also make them slant forward or back, depending on which way it wants to go.

When the weather is warm and there is plenty of food and moisture, earthworms usually stay quite near the surface of the soil. When winter comes, they plug up the mouth of the burrow and crawl down into its deepest part. Often several

The earthworm moves without legs by stretching out and then thickening part of its body to wedge itself in its tunnel.

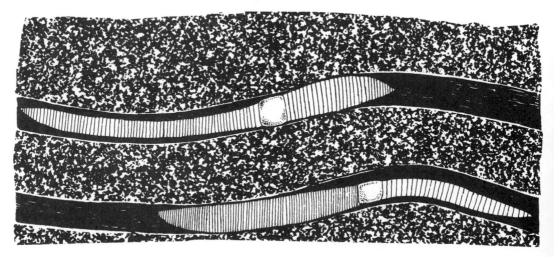

earthworms spend the winter in the bottom of a tunnel in the soil, curled up together in a ball.

Earthworms are soft and juicy, and they have many enemies. Moles tunnel after them, and skunks dig them out of their burrows. Smaller soil dwellers, like certain slugs, also hunt them. Birds, especially owls and robins, eat enormous numbers of earthworms and feed them to their young. When people interfere with this cycle of nature, there can be some unexpected effects. In Ann Arbor, Michigan, for example, insecticides were sprayed on elm trees to kill bark beetles. The elm leaves that fell to the ground in the autumn were full of poison. Earthworms pulled them down into the soil and ate them. The poison did not seem to bother the worms, but more and more of it built up in their bodies as they ate the leaves. In the spring, when the robins came, they ate the poison-filled worms. And soon the robins died.

The soft-bodied earthworms have an unusual defense against their enemies. If a predator bites off a piece of an earthworm, the rest of the worm may wriggle away safely. And, depending on which part was cut off, the worm may be able to grow it back again. Many people think that if you cut an earthworm in half, each half will be able to grow back the missing parts, and there will be two new earthworms. This is not exactly true. An earthworm usually has about 150 sections, or segments, along its body. If part or even all of the first ten segments are cut off, the earthworm will be able to grow back about four or five of these front segments. Then it will be a perfectly healthy worm, although perhaps a bit shorter than normal. This seems quite surprising, since this front part of the earthworm contains its brain! Earthworms can regrow much more of the tail end. But if the worm is cut between segments numbers 11 to 36, it will almost surely die.

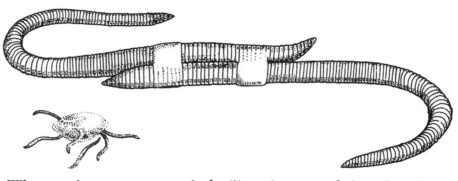

When earthworms mate, each fertilizes the eggs of the other. The eggs are placed in a lemon-shaped cocoon, where the young worms develop.

An earthworm is both male and female at the same time! But it cannot have babies by itself; it needs a mate. When two earthworms mate, each of them becomes both a father and a mother.

On a warm, humid night, two earthworms of about the same size meet while they are crawling about on the surface of the soil outside their burrows. The two worms lie close together with their heads pointing in opposite directions. As they press their bodies together, each worm gives some male seeds, sperms, to the other. Then they part and crawl back into their own burrows.

The sperms that the earthworm has received from its mate are stored in a special bag inside its body until it is ready to lay its eggs. After a while, the worm forms a slimy ring about its body. Carefully it wriggles backward out of this slimy tube, placing first the sperms and then its eggs inside. After the worm is out, the tube pinches together on the ends and forms a lemon-shaped cocoon.

Inside the cocoon, the eggs join with the sperms, and baby earthworms begin to form. Soon they are miniature copies of their parents. They break out of the cocoon and begin their life in the soil.

Earthworms have an enormous effect on the soil and the creatures that live in it. They are nature's plows. Naturalists have estimated that there can be as many as 190,000 in an acre of soil. That means that you may find up to 30 earthworms in your bucket of soil, depending on where you collected it. The largest numbers are found in gardens and the fewest in wastelands.

These earthworms can live for up to ten years, and they tirelessly churn through the soil, digging their burrows and searching for food. They help to loosen the soil and help to mix food materials and minerals with the soil particles. The soil earthworms have loosened can hold oxygen from the air, and moisture, much better than hard-packed soil. It provides homes and food for many smaller soil animals and better conditions in which plants can grow.

Earthworms may help to turn the soil over just as a plow does. Some earthworms leave their castings inside their burrows. But the common earthworm, which Charles Darwin studied about a century ago, comes out of its burrow to leave some of its castings on the surface. Darwin covered some soil with a layer of red sand. After seven years (scientists who study nature sometimes have to be extremely patient and persistent!) he found that the layer of red sand was covered with two inches of soil that earthworms had brought up from their burrows. Two inches may not seem like very much, but in your lifetime these earthworms could bring up a layer of new soil nearly two feet deep.

The fact that earthworms are shy of light makes them rather difficult to study. To add to the problem, they seem to need to be touched on all sides of their bodies. This makes them crawl into narrow cracks and gaps in the soil. Naturalists have figured out a way to solve these problems. They put their earthworms in a cage made out of two sheets of glass with a thin layer of soil between them and watch the worms in very dim light or in red light. Although earthworms are sensitive to light, they seem to be blind to red light.

Many interesting experiments can be conducted in an earthworm cage of this kind. You can study what earthworms like best to eat by placing various kinds of leaves and other foods on top of the layer of soil. You can sprinkle a layer of sand on top of the soil and watch how it becomes covered by a layer of soil, just as Darwin did. You can even place various other soil animals and plants in the earthworm cage and study how the earthworms' activity helps them to grow and multiply.

An earthworm cage. The solid glass walls give the worms a feeling of security, while the observer can still watch them tunneling, feeding, and mating.

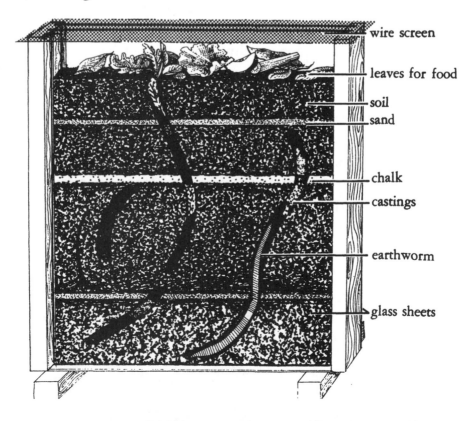

wire screen

leaves for food

soil

sand

chalk

castings

earthworm

glass sheets

Roundworms
THREADLIKE WRIGGLERS

IF YOU SPREAD OUT A SPOONFUL OF SOIL FROM YOUR BUCKET AND look through it carefully, you will probably find a number of creatures that look like tiny white threads. They do not lie limply like bits of sewing thread; instead they wriggle and thrash about. These are roundworms. They look so much like tiny threads that the scientific name of their group, Nematoda, comes from a Greek word meaning thread.

There are enormous numbers of roundworms in the world of life beneath our feet. There may be millions in a single bucket of soil. Indeed, the vast multitude of roundworms in our world has prompted one zoologist to some fanciful imagining. If all the matter in the earth *except* the nematodes were suddenly to vanish, he has written, our planet would still be outlined in an eerie way. A thin film of soil roundworms would trace the contours of the hills and valleys. Roundworm parasites would outline the forms of trees and bushes, animals, and even people.

A roundworm is a very simple-looking creature. Its body looks like a long, slim tube, pointed at each end. It is covered with a thick, tough layer called a cuticle. It does not have a very efficient set of muscles. As a result, the roundworm can only thrash back and forth, moving through the soil or the body of some other creature by pushing against solid surfaces

31

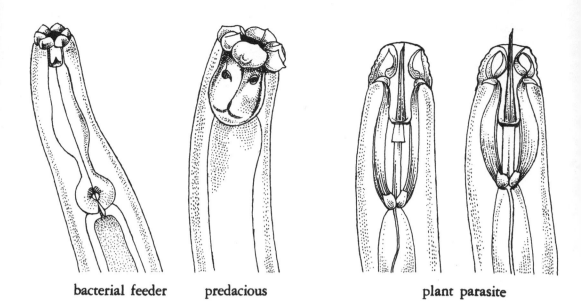

bacterial feeder   predacious   plant parasite

Roundworms have specialized mouthparts, suited to their way of life.

to propel itself along. Many of the smaller roundworms are transparent, so that the organs of their bodies can be seen through the cuticle. Others are white or yellowish.

At the front tip of the roundworm's body is its mouth. It may have sucking lips or cutting teeth or piercing needles, depending on the kind of food it eats.

Nematodes find a variety of food in the soil. The smallest ones (so small that fifty lined up end-to-end would cover only an inch) feed on microscopic bacteria and minute algae, a very simple kind of plant. Larger soil roundworms live on tiny soil animals, such as protozoa and rotifers, and on smaller roundworms. These nematode hunters have sharp teeth or grinding plates to mince up their prey.

These free-living roundworms are found mostly in the top two inches of soil. They are very well equipped against one of the greatest dangers of living near the surface of the soil— drying out. When their soil home grows too dry, roundworms

32

withdraw into a sort of sleeping state. They shrink inside their skin, which remains as a kind of protective shell. They do not move or feed. They do not seem to be alive at all. While the roundworms rest, safe inside their protective cases, their light bodies may be picked up by the wind with bits of dusty soil and carried to new homes. Then, when it rains and there is enough moisture again, they come to life once more.

Many of the nematodes in the soil spend at least part of their lives as parasites inside the bodies of plants or animals. Various kinds of eelworms, for example, attack the roots, stems, or leaves of plants. Male and female worms feed and mate and give birth to enormous numbers of young worms. Many of the young remain inside the plant in which they were born, sucking its juices and growing and mating in their turn. Other young eelworms slip out into the soil and travel through it to attack new plants. When many eelworms are feeding on a plant, it may wilt and die. Farmers often find that when the same crop has been grown in a field for a number of years, the plants become sickly. Yet if a different crop is planted in the same field, it grows quite well. One reason for this is that one type of plant may take certain chemicals and food materials out of the soil, while another kind of plant may replace them. But in many cases crop rotation—planting one crop in a field one year and a different one the next—works because the sickly plants had become infested with roundworms. These worms often can live only in a particular kind of plant. When there are no plants of that kind around, the worms remain in the soil in a resting state and may eventually die.

Some nematode parasites live in the bodies of beetles, earth-

Roundworm parasites infest plants and animals.

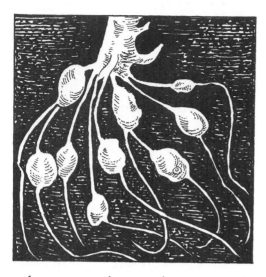

eelworm parasites causing root malformation

eelworm parasites causing rotting
cross section of an onion (dark parts
are rotted)

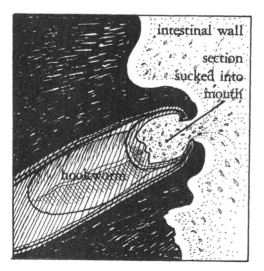

cross section of mouth of hookworm
attached to intestinal wall

cyst of trichina worm in muscle of pig

worms, and other soil animals. Others spend part of their lives feeding inside the bodies of large animals and even humans. They reach the soil with the body wastes of their hosts, remain there for a time, and then may find a new host. Eggs or worms may cling to vegetables or other food that is eaten without being washed thoroughly, or they may be washed by the rains into drinking water. Some roundworm parasites have even more ingenious ways of finding new hosts. The young form of the hookworm, for example, lives in the soil and then bores through the skin of the feet or ankles of a human to enter the body of its new host. There it lives in the intestines, sucking in blood and juices from the intestinal wall. Until quite recently, a combination of outdoor toilets and the practice of going about barefoot made this roundworm an important health problem in the south-eastern United States.

Snails and Slugs
SLIME GLIDERS

IN RECENT YEARS, SOME PEOPLE HAVE BECOME VERY CONCERNED about the effects of chemical pesticides on the living world. These chemicals can pollute the soil and water, and the residues they leave on foods can be harmful to the people who eat them, besides harming the farmworkers who harvest them. Scientists are trying to find effective ways to control farm and garden pests without adding to the pollution of our earth, and "organic" foods, grown without the use of pesticides, have become very popular. The problems involved are often difficult, but sometimes the answers turn out to be surprisingly simple. Shrewd gardeners have known for years, for example, that shallow pans filled with stale beer make fine traps for slugs. The slugs smell the beer, crawl up into the pans, and drown.

Both slugs and snails are mollusks, relatives of oysters, clams, octopuses, and squids. The smaller group to which slugs and snails belong is called Gastropoda, which means "belly foot." The reason for this name becomes quite clear as soon as you watch a snail or slug moving. It glides along by the movement of a single large, flat, muscular foot on the underside of its body. It produces a thick, slimy substance that helps it to slip along easily over the roughest terrain. In fact, a slug can even glide over the sharp edge of an upturned razor blade without getting hurt—it is protected by its thick slime. The slime trails that snails and slugs leave behind them stretch out in a shining ribbon until bits of dust and dirt stick to the slime and cover it over.

Land snails carry the same kind of coiled shell on their

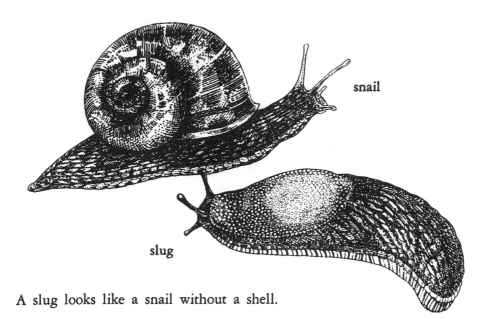

snail

slug

A slug looks like a snail without a shell.

backs as their ocean-dwelling relatives. Many of them can pull their bodies completely inside the shell, with the tough bottom of the foot blocking the doorway. When winter comes, some land snails glue the edge of their shell to a tree trunk or some other solid surface and hibernate until spring. But the shells of land snails are often lighter and more easily broken than those of their ocean relatives.

A slug looks like a snail without a shell. It can stretch its soft body out and thus become thin enough to squeeze through narrow cracks and burrows in the soil.

Land snails and slugs have a pair of eyes, each at the end of a long, thin tentacle growing from the top of the head. If anything touches one of these eyestalks, it quickly turns inside out, like the finger of a glove, pulling the eye in to safety. But if an enemy bites off an eyestalk, the snail or slug does not remain a cripple for the rest of its life. It can grow a new one.

Sea snails and slugs breathe through gills very much like the gills of a fish. But their land relatives have breathing organs like lungs, and they can breathe air just as we do.

37

Most land snails and slugs are vegetarians. They may feed on decaying plant matter and help to break it down into smaller bits that will later become part of the soil. Or they may attack living plants and can be real garden pests. They rasp away at leaves or stems with a sawlike tongue called a radula. Each kind of slug or snail has its own particular shape and arrangement of the "teeth" on the edges of its radula, and scientists can recognize the different types according to the patterns these cutting tongues leave.

If your bucket of soil contained several kinds of snails or slugs, there is a simple way to make a collection of radula patterns. Melt some cooking fat, pour a layer of melted fat into large jar lids, and allow it to cool. Now you will have a layer of solid fat in the inside of each lid. Place each snail or slug in a separate, clean one-pound jam or applesauce jar with a few drops of water, and cover it loosely with one of the fat-coated lids. Within a day or two the snail or slug will crawl up and leave its tongue marks in the fat on the lid.

Land snails and slugs are easy to raise, and many interesting experiments can be conducted with them. You can try feeding them various kinds of foods and see which ones they eat, which

Radula patterns can be collected on a fat-coated jar lid.

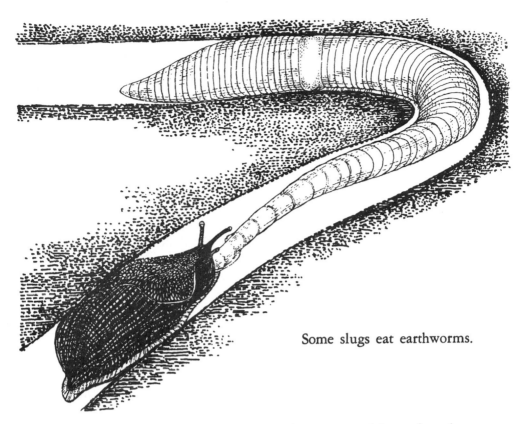

Some slugs eat earthworms.

they seem to like most, how much they eat, and how fast they grow. Some may eat only dead leaves. Others may prefer fresh vegetables or young plant seedlings. Some snails or slugs may even eat meat. Indeed, although most of these land mollusks are vegetarians, some will eat anything, and some are even carnivorous. One kind of slug, for example, specializes in hunting earthworms. It can stretch out thin to squeeze through earthworm burrows, searching for its favorite prey. Its radula has large teeth that seize the soft body of the earthworm. If this slug happens to meet an earthworm head-on in its burrow, it clamps on, and a fierce tug-of-war follows. The earthworm contracts as hard as it can, trying to pull away. But the slug holds on tightly, and it contracts its body too. If the earthworm is larger than the slug, it may drag the predator along through the burrow, but the slug does not let go. Although this slug prefers earthworms, it will eat other soil animals as well (even other slugs) and may also come out of the soil to hunt its prey on the surface.

Researchers who were trying to find a way to control a snail that is a troublesome crop pest discovered that its worst enemy is another snail, a carnivorous one. They hope that breeding large numbers of the carnivorous snails and releasing them in the field will make it possible to wipe out the pests.

Snails and slugs have a number of enemies in addition to the members of their own group. They are large enough to be a tempting mouthful for a bird, a mouse, or various other animals of forest and field. Some soil dwellers also prey on land gastropods. One group of daddy longlegs, relatives of the spiders, eats nothing but snails. After eating up a snail with her sharp jaws, the female of this daddy longlegs species lays her eggs inside the empty shell. A number of beetles also eat snails. One kind has a long pointed mouth that can reach into the snail's shell without having to break it open. Young fireflies, the larvae of beetles, feed mainly on snails.

The mating of land snails and slugs is fascinating. Like earthworms, these creatures are hermaphrodites: each individual is both male and female. Field slugs come out on the surface to mate in the early morning or evening. They eat each other's slime and coil their bodies together. Each slug transfers the male seeds, or sperm, to the other. Then, within a few weeks, each slug becomes a mother, laying a few dozen pearly white eggs in the soil. The eggs hatch in about a month, and the young slugs look like tiny copies of their parents. After a few months (or longer, depending on the time of year they were born) they are old enough to mate. The adult slugs continue to grow, and they live for about a year and a half.

Wood Lice
ARMORED SCAVENGERS

YOU WOULD NOT EXPECT TO FIND ANY LOBSTERS OR SHRIMPS IN your bucket of soil, for these are water animals. They belong to a group of many-legged creatures called crustaceans. Yet one of the close relatives of these sea dwellers is a true land animal. Indeed, it is so common that you are likely to find it hiding under almost any rock or bit of rotting wood or bark on the surface of the soil, especially if there are plenty of dead leaves and other vegetation about.

These land crustaceans are wood lice. They belong to a group that scientists call Isopoda, which means "equal legs"— for all of their seven pairs of legs are about the same length. Their long oval bodies are covered by a rounded coat of armor made of a series of hard, smooth plates that fit together like the links of an expansion watchband. On the front of the wood louse's head, two long, curved "feelers," or antennae, constantly move about, testing the environment.

The wood louse leads a quiet life, more often on the soil than inside it. It hides under rocks and logs and comes out to feed on bits of decaying plants. When wood lice are plentiful, they have a great effect on the lives of other soil animals, for they help to break down plant matter into smaller bits that the tiny animals of the soil can feed upon.

You will not need a magnifying glass to see the wood lice in your soil sample or any special device to capture them.

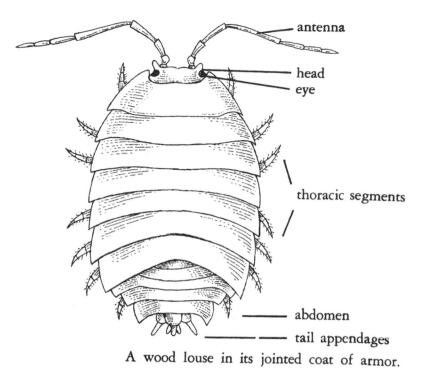

antenna

head
eye

thoracic segments

abdomen
tail appendages

A wood louse in its jointed coat of armor.

These many-legged animals are among the larger soil dwellers. They grow to three quarters of an inch or longer.

Although the peaceful wood louse is one of the "giants" of the world of the soil, he has a number of enemies. Spiders may snare or sting him. A bird may swoop down and snatch him up from the surface of the soil with a snap of its beak. Wood lice do have a number of defenses. Many of them have special glands along the sides of the body. If they are attacked, a sticky, nasty-smelling liquid oozes out of these glands. This "chemical warfare" may make a hungry spider change its mind and back away. The wood louse's coat of armor also helps to protect him from enemies. But this armor is only a half shell. It covers his back, but leaves his softer belly open. It would seem that all an enemy would have to do would be to flip him over and his armor would be of no help at all.

Some wood lice, the pill bugs, have solved this problem

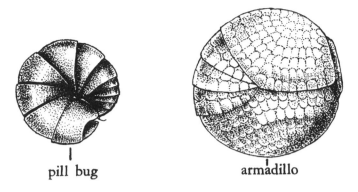

pill bug   armadillo

Many armored animals curl up into a ball when danger threatens.

very handily. If they are in danger, they pull in their legs and antennae and curl up into a tight ball. Now the wood louse looks like a little round pill, with nothing to be seen but neatly fitting plates of armor. After a while, when the enemy has probably given up and gone away, the pill bug uncurls and scurries away.

Scientists who studied pill bugs were amazed at how much they resemble a very different kind of animal, the armadillo of South America. This large mammal also has a coat of armor, and when it is attacked it curls up into a ball so that its soft belly is protected. And so the group of pill bugs was given the name *Armadillidium*.

It is said that some dogs and other clever predators that hunt armadillos learn to roll them into a river or a pool. Gasping for breath, the armadillo uncurls, and then the predator pounces. This technique would not work very well for a pill bug, for it does not mind the water at all. Indeed, like its water-dwelling relatives, it breathes through organs that are very much like the gills of fish. These breathing organs have to be kept moist all the time in order to work properly. And so it is not surprising that pill bugs and other wood lice stay in damp places. They have an amazing "moisture sense." If you place a wood louse in a container in which the air is too dry (it prefers more than 90 percent humidity—about the wetness of a muggy summer day), it moves about restlessly. It seems to be searching for something. If you then place a water-soaked cotton wad in one corner of the container, the wood louse will immediately scurry toward the moist spot and settle down there.

The pill bug's suit of armor provides fine protection, but it causes problems too. It is heavy and awkward, and because it is hardened into shape, it cannot grow. In order for a pill bug to grow, it must shed its skin, or molt. Hiding in a crack in the soil, it wriggles out of its hard old skin, and there is a soft new one underneath. It puffs up its body as much as it can, so that when the new skin hardens it will provide more room to grow.

The pill bug is not the only animal that must shed its skin in order to grow. Its relatives, lobsters, shrimps, and crabs, also molt. So do all insects. But there is something quite odd about the way the pill bug molts. It sheds the front half of its old skin first. Then some time goes by—perhaps even two weeks—before it sheds the back half. Look at the pill bugs

Cutaway diagram of the wood louse, showing the brood pouch.

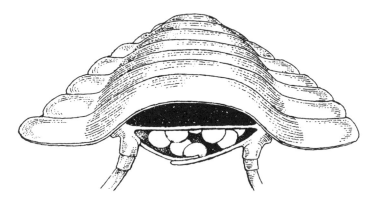

you have found in your bucket of soil. Most of them are probably dark gray. But there may be a few that seem to be two different colors, one half light and the other dark. They are probably right in the middle of molting.

Some of your wood lice may be carrying about a bulging bag formed by flat plates growing out of several pairs of legs. This is a brood pouch, and it is full of eggs. The mother wood louse carries her eggs about with her until they are ready to hatch. The baby wood lice look like miniature copies of their mother. But if you look very closely, you will see some important differences. They are paler, and they have only six pairs of legs instead of seven. They do not grow the seventh pair of legs until their first molt.

During spring, summer, and fall, wood lice scurry busily about, feeding on dead plants and sometimes even eating living ones as well. Many kinds are active only at night, but the pill bugs sometimes venture out in the daytime too. They do not need to fear the sunlight as much as their relatives, for their armor helps to keep them from drying out. When the cold of winter comes, wood lice crawl into sheltering cracks and crannies to stay there in a quiet state until spring.

Centipedes and Millipedes
MANY-LEGGED CRAWLERS

IF YOU HAD A DOZEN LEGS, HOW WOULD YOU KNOW WHICH FOOT to put forward next? It seems as though it would be a hopelessly confusing problem to walk without tripping over your own feet. Yet wood lice, with fourteen legs, seem to manage very nicely. And some creatures of the soil are equipped with dozens and even hundreds of legs! These are the centipedes and millipedes.

The name centipede means "hundred legs," but actually many of the common members of this group have only about fifteen pairs of legs. The name of the millipedes is an exaggeration too: it means "thousand legs," but even the longest "thousand leggers" have only two hundred legs, and most have far fewer.

For some time scientists grouped both centipedes and millipedes in a single group, the myriapods ("many legs"). It is true that both groups have long, wormlike bodies with many segments and many pairs of legs. Each has a pair of antennae and eyes on the sides of its head. But there are a number of important differences between them.

The easiest way to tell the difference between a centipede and a millipede (if it will hold still long enough) is to notice how the animal's legs are arranged along its body. A centipede has just a single pair of legs attached to each segment of its body.

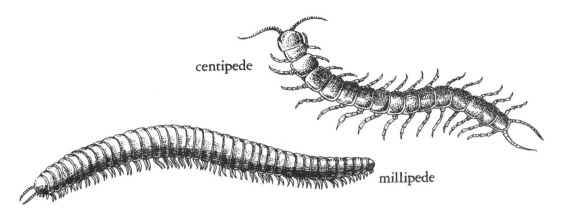

centipede

millipede

Millipedes have two pairs of legs on each segment, while centipedes have only one pair.

Each segment of a millipede's body has two pairs of legs attached to it.

Another difference that is easy to spot is the way the animals move. For although both centipedes and millipedes always know which foot to put forward next, the two groups have solved the problem in different ways. Centipedes seem to wriggle along, because the legs of each pair alternate. First one moves, and then the other. Millipedes seem to glide along smoothly, as waves of movement pass down the body from one pair of legs to the next.

Centipedes and millipedes also have very different ways of life. Centipedes are carnivorous. They are hunters of the world of the soil. They hide in the damp cracks under stones and bark and come out at night to prowl about, searching for juicy insects, slugs, or worms to eat. The first pair of legs is a special set of hunter's tools—a pair of poison claws with sharp tips that can pierce the centipede's prey like needles and inject a dose of poison. (Centipedes may bite humans if they are handled roughly. Their bite is like a wasp's sting.)

Centipedes have a group of tiny eyes on each side of the head, but they do not use their sense of sight to find their prey.

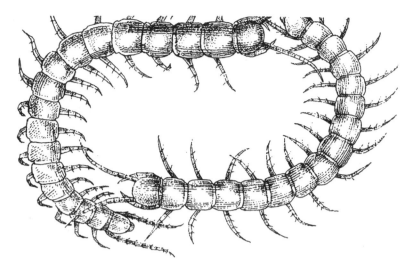

Centipedes have a complicated courtship dance.

It is dark when they are about, so they find their prey by touch. The centipede hunter prowls, feeling constantly in every direction with its antennae. Its body is rather flat because its legs are attached on the sides, and it can squeeze through narrow cracks with ease. As soon as its searching antennae touch something that feels like prey, snap! go the poison claws.

Centipedes tend to avoid light, scurrying away into darkness whenever they can. Scientists have found that these animals flee from light even when they have been "blindfolded," their eyes covered with heavy paint. So they seem to have some sort of "light sense" in their skin as well. This sense helps to keep the centipedes under cover, where they are protected from enemies and from drying out. But avoiding light is not all that helps to protect centipedes. They are very sensitive to touch all over their bodies, and they seem most content when as many parts of the body as possible are in contact with something solid. This is shown by a very simple experiment. If a centipede is placed in a smooth dish in very dim light, it will run about restlessly. If it comes to rest at all, it will do so at the edge, where two sides of its body are in contact with the dish. But if a small piece of glass tubing is placed in the dish with the centipede, it will soon crawl inside and settle down peacefully.

Centipedes come in two sexes, just as humans do. They have a complicated courtship. A male and a female meet in a narrow passage in the soil. They touch each other with their antennae and may move about in a sort of dance. Then the male spins a web across the passage, and in it he places a packet of sperms. Now he signals to the female with his antennae and slowly moves away. She follows him over the web and picks up the packet of sperms. Inside the female's body, the sperms join with eggs to start the lives of new baby centipedes.

Some mother centipedes lay their eggs in the soil and then go off and leave them. But others lay clusters of eggs and may even care for them. The mother may coil her body tightly around the eggs, so that they cannot be seen from the outside. Now and then she unwinds, picks up an egg in two pairs of legs, and licks it. Scientists believe she is licking off the spores of molds that might grow on the egg and kill it. If an egg falls out of the cluster, she will pick it up and put it back. And if an enemy tries to eat any of the eggs, she will attack him fiercely.

Some baby centipedes are born with all their legs. But others are born with only seven pairs of legs; more are added each

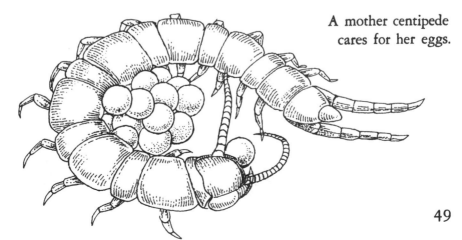

A mother centipede
cares for her eggs.

time the growing centipede molts. Some centipedes raised in the laboratory have lived for several years.

The millipedes live a very different kind of life from that of the fierce centipedes. Nearly all of them are vegetarians. They live mainly on rotting plant matter, although some will feed on living molds and some even attack growing plants and seeds.

Most millipedes can burrow through the soil. They cannot eat their way along as the earthworms do. Instead, some use their hard bodies to push their way through the earth, like battering rams. Other types, with flat, wedge-shaped heads, cut their way through the soil like a knife. Young millipedes seem to be too small to dig burrows in these ways. They must get along with the cracks and tunnels that are already there.

The ability to scurry into a handy burrow or crack in the soil helps to protect millipedes from some of their enemies above ground, like birds and mice. They also have unusual defenses against the insect hunters of the world of the soil. Along the sides of the millipede's body are two rows of "stink glands." These glands produce a bad-smelling substance that can frighten away insect predators or even kill them, for it contains small amounts of the deadly poison cyanide. Millipedes are quite safe for a human to handle, though. The small amount of poison is not enough to harm a person, and even a mouse would not get sick unless it ate too many millipedes.

Some millipedes play dead when they are attacked. Long

A millipede rams its way through the soil.

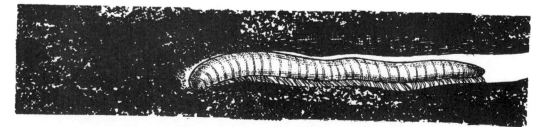

The pill millipede faces danger in much
the same way as the wood louse (see page 43).

ones may curl up like watch springs, with the hard armor on
their backs turned upward. The pill millipede looks very much
like a pill bug, and it too curls up into a round ball when it is
disturbed.

Some male millipedes spin webs when they mate, much as
the centipedes do. They may also lay down long straight
"roads" of a sticky substance to guide the female to the web.
Other male millipedes hand their sperm packets to the females
with special pairs of legs.

One of the most common kinds of millipede takes care of her
eggs. She mixes her saliva with earth to build a dome-shaped
nest. Then she lays her eggs through a hole in the top and seals
up the nest when she is finished. Often she may be found
curled up around her nest.

When the young millipedes hatch out, they have only a few
segments, but they add more each time they molt. Molting may
take place in a special nest, where the millipede can hide until
its new coat of armor hardens. Millipedes continue to molt and
grow, adding a few segments at a time, for their entire lives.
Most live a year or two; some types live up to seven years.

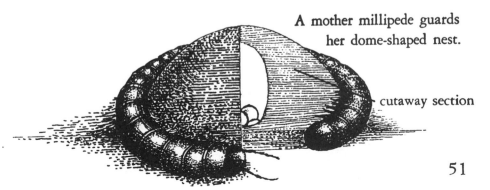

A mother millipede guards
her dome-shaped nest.

cutaway section

Springtails
SWARMING LEAPERS

IF YOU TRIED TO COUNT ALL OF THE CREATURES IN YOUR BUCKET-
ful of soil it would probably take you weeks. For there are
thousands or even millions of them. You would probably find
that most of them belonged to one of three main groups:
roundworms, mites, and springtails.

Springtails are a kind of insect. They are found on all the
lands of the earth from the Arctic to the Antarctic. There are
probably more springtails alive today than all the other
insects combined. When you realize that there are more than
a million different kinds of insects and only a few thousand
different kinds of springtails, this seems amazing.

To see the springtails from your bucket clearly, you will need
a magnifying glass, for most of them are less than a quarter of
an inch long. Like all the other insects, springtails have bodies
that are divided into three parts, a head, a thorax, and an abdomen. Three pairs of legs are attached to the middle part, or
thorax, and a single pair of thin, jointed feelers, or antennae,
grow out from the front of the head. The bodies of some
springtails are long and slim and clearly divided into segments,
like the links on an expansion watchband. Others are plump
and pear shaped, and the marks of the segments cannot be
seen. The springtails that live at the top of the soil have a pair
of fairly good eyes. But those that spend their whole lives in the

The springtail's spring is a handy escape device.

darkness of the lower layers of soil have no eyes at all and are completely blind.

Springtails get their name from a structure at the end of their bodies. It is a long, branched tail, shaped something like a two-tined fork. This tail does not hang down as the tails of most other animals do. Instead, it is held under the small insect's body, attached by a special catch on the underside of his abdomen. This catch has two sets of tiny teeth that hook onto the two prongs of the spring and hold it tightly closed. When a stalking ant creeps up on a springtail and is about to eat him, the tiny insect may not have time to run away. But he has another way to escape. Suddenly the catch lets go, and the tail springs powerfully backward. Like a rock from a slingshot, the springtail is launched straight up in the air. He can leap as high as several inches. This may not seem very far, but it is many times the length of his tiny body and is enough to send him high over the head of the startled ant.

Not all springtail species have a spring. This elegant escape mechanism would not work very well deep within the soil. An insect that tried to use it would probably quickly bump his head and bounce back down into the jaws of the enemy he was trying to escape. Only springtail species that live at the top of the soil have a long spring. The tails of the springtails that live

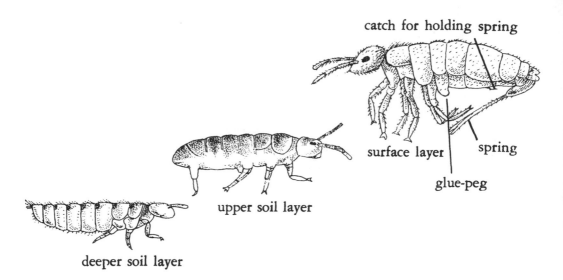

catch for holding spring

surface layer

spring

glue-peg

upper soil layer

deeper soil layer

Different types of springtails are found at different depths in the soil.

a few inches down in the soil are somewhat shorter, and their antennae are shorter too. The blind springtails that live deep within the soil have very short antennae and no springs at all.

The group of springtails has another name, which scientists often use: Collembola. This name comes from Greek words that mean "glue-peg." The springtail's "glue-peg" is a tube that grows down from the underside of the insect's abdomen. A sticky kind of glue is made in the tube and helps the springtail to cling to smooth surfaces, such as a stone or the stem or root of a plant.

Scientists believe that the "glue-peg" has another, even more important job to do. Springtails live in damp places, and they need moisture to survive. Most of them breathe through their thin skin, and they take in the oxygen that is dissolved in the film of moisture on the outside of their bodies. If they dry out, they will die. In the laboratory, scientists have watched springtails dipping their "glue-pegs" into droplets of moisture. The drier the air is, the more often they "drink" this way. If a little colored dye is added to the water, the color can be seen going into the insect's body through the tube. Some springtails can stretch their "glue-pegs" out into a long, thin tube that reaches all the way to the mouth. With this long tube a springtail may transfer water to his mouth or even clean himself.

Springtails are very clean little animals, even though we tend to think of the world they live in as rather dirty. They are constantly cleaning themselves, like housecats. From his mouth the springtail takes a shining drop of liquid. Holding the precious drop in the claws of one of his forelegs, he scrubs his head, antennae, and legs. He cannot reach his whole body, so he may transfer the drop carefully to one of his second pair of legs, farther down his body. If the droplet does not break during the springtail's bath, he thriftily swallows it when he is finished.

The springtails that live in the lower parts of the soil are usually pale and whitish, but those that live near or at the surface may be gray or brown or even brightly colored. Yellow, green, blue, lavender, and red springtails have been found. Some are speckled or striped, or have other vivid patterns. Scientists believe the color patterns of the springtails that live at the surface of the soil may help them to survive. Some of them look very much like small spiders that live in the leaf

A springtail washes itself like a cat.

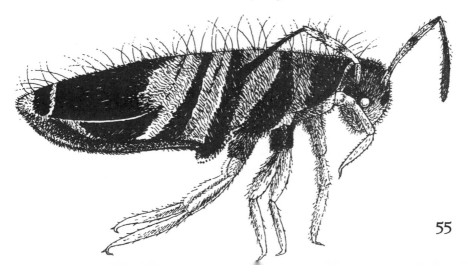

mold. Few animals will attack a spider, which may give a deadly bite, and so they leave the spiderlike springtails alone too. Other springtails use a kind of "chemical warfare" against their enemies. Their blood contains some chemicals that are bad-tasting or poisonous to predators like ants and mites, and if they are attacked, blood oozes out of tiny openings in their skin. This "bleeding" occurs even before the springtail has been hurt. A chemical defense of this kind is not very effective if the predator finds out his prey is not good to eat after he has already killed it. The bright-colored patterns act as warning signals. Once an ant or mite has tried to eat a bad-tasting springtail, it learns not to touch that kind again.

The bright colors of some species of springtails may be produced by colored pigments in their skin. Other species have an overlay of scales, very much like the colored scales on a butterfly's wings. These scales are very slippery and help springtails to escape from their enemies. They help these insects to slip out of an ant's grasp and may also help them to get free when they are trapped in spider webs spun close to the ground. A springtail that has accidentally run or leaped into a spider web may turn and thrash about. The scales on his body are not very tightly attached. They tear off and stick to the strands of the spider web, and the springtail slips away, leaving his lost scales behind.

The main enemies of springtails are ants. One group of hunting ants seems to be specially equipped for catching this leaping prey. Their enormous jaws can gape so wide that they are almost in a straight line. The ant creeps along with her jaws wide open and two long hairs sticking out of the front of her head. When the two feelers touch the ant's prey, her jaws immediately snap shut onto the helpless springtail. If the

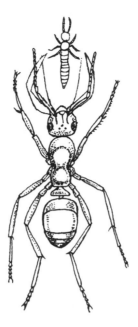

With jaws gaping open, an ant sneaks up on an unsuspecting springtail.

springtail tries to use his spring to jump away, the ant immediately lifts him off the ground and paralyzes him with a sting.

The springtails themselves live quietly in the soil, feeding on fallen leaves or fungi or the droppings of other soil animals. Their mouthparts are made for biting or sucking and are kept folded up in small pouches in the head when they are not feeding. A few springtails eat tender plant seedlings and are garden pests. Others feed on tiny roundworms. These worms may be almost as long as the springtail himself. He grasps the wriggling worm by one end and sucks it in the way some people suck in long strings of spaghetti.

· Some springtails mate in a peculiar way. The male does not place his sex cells, or sperms, inside the female's body. Instead, he sends them out in tiny droplets of moisture, which he attaches to the ground with a thin, short stem. He may place these droplets in a circle around the female, like a ring of

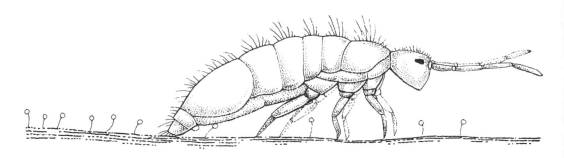

A female springtail picks up a sperm droplet.

lollipops standing up on their sticks; or he may scatter them around in a place that females are likely to visit, so thickly that they look like a tiny garden of molds. Sooner or later, a female springtail will blunder into one of the sperm droplets and will take it up into an opening at the tip of her abdomen. There, inside her body, the sperms of the male will join with her own sex cells.

Within a few days the female lays a small cluster of tiny, glistening eggs. These eggs take in moisture from the soil and swell up. Then the outer shell bursts, and the baby springtails develop inside the thin inner membrane of the egg. A few days later they hatch, looking like tiny copies of their parents. Like other insects, they must shed their skin, or molt, in order to grow.

Normally we are not aware of the springtails living in the soil. Indeed, these animals were not even discovered until the magnifying glass was invented. But sometimes they begin to multiply wildly and swarm up out of the ground in enormous numbers. Large patches consisting of thousands or millions of springtails may suddenly appear at the edges of ponds, on tree trunks, or in fields and gardens. They may even swarm up onto the top of the snow during a winter thaw. They climb up from the soil through small spaces around the stems of weeds and shrubs. When bad weather comes again, some go back down the same way, but many others try to force their way down through the packed snow and die. The springtails in these winter swarms are often called snow fleas, but they do not seem to belong to any one special kind. Instead they seem to be the ordinary kinds of springtails, which for some mysterious reason have left their homes in the soil.

Why do the springtails swarm? Scientists are not sure. These tiny insects can have enormous numbers of young, and if conditions are just right for them to feed and grow and there are not too many of their natural enemies about, they may have a sort of "population explosion." Their home in the soil grows very crowded. Scientists have found that crowding causes many animals to begin to behave peculiarly, and springtails are no exception. When they are swarming, they tend to run toward bright lights instead of away from them as springtails normally do. And they may even begin to fight and eat each other.

Some scientists are now becoming concerned about the human "population explosion" and fear that our world is growing too crowded. They think we should study animals like springtails to find out why crowding makes them behave so strangely. Perhaps these inhabitants of the cities in the soil have some lessons for us to learn.

Spiders and Their Relatives
LURKING HUNTERS

THERE IS A FLASH OF EMERALD GREEN AGAINST THE SOIL AS A tiger beetle scurries along, hunting caterpillars for his dinner. He spots one crawling up the stem of a nearby plant. But as he closes in for the attack, he does not notice the edge of a spider web and blunders right into it. The beetle struggles to pull away, but his legs are tangled in the sticky threads. As soon as he tears one free, another is caught.

Spider silk is strong, but the beetle is large. With enough time he could free himself. But he does not have much time at all. His first struggles send vibrations traveling along the web, like messages along a telegraph wire. Perched on a platform at the center, the mistress of the web feels these vibrations. Quickly she races along the spokes of the web to the spot where the beetle is struggling. His strong, pointed jaws snap at her. Keeping at a safe distance, the spider shoots out silk from special silk-making glands at the end of her abdomen. Carefully she wraps her struggling prey in a shining silken "straitjacket" that holds him firmly. Now she dares to come closer. With her two pointed fangs she bites the beetle and injects a bit of poison with each fang. This spider venom quiets the beetle, and it contains chemicals that begin to digest the spider's victim, right inside its own shell. For the spider does not have chewing mouthparts, as many other animals do. She digests her meals *before* she eats them, and later sucks in the liquid food

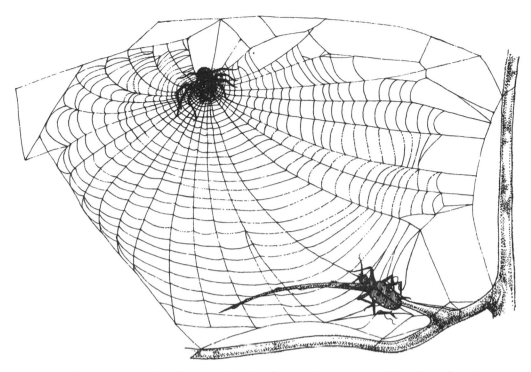

The beetle struggles, but it is already caught in the sticky threads of the spider web.

with a sort of sucking stomach. After she has finished with the beetle, only his empty shell will remain.

Many people think spiders are insects. Actually they are not, although they are related to insects. There are many differences between spiders and insects, some of which can easily be seen just by looking at them closely.

Insects have six legs. (They may have one or two pairs of wings in addition.) Spiders have eight legs used for walking. In addition, they have a pair of clawlike structures in front of the mouth, which are the poison fangs. Another pair of structures attached behind the mouth may be used as "feelers." Spiders do not have antennae, as insects do. Their eyes are not as good as the eyes of insects either, even though they have quite a number of them. Spiders usually have *eight* eyes, but they are very tiny.

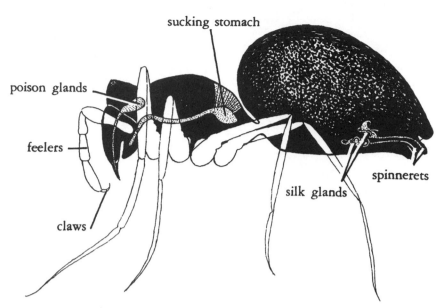

A typical spider. Compare its body parts with those of the ant on page 84.

An insect's body is usually clearly divided into three parts, which often look like beads on a string. In front is the head, which holds the eyes, antennae, and mouth. Then comes the trunk, or thorax, to which the legs and wings are attached. The third part is the abdomen. A spider's body is divided into only two parts. In front is the cephalothorax (which means "head-trunk"); behind is the abdomen. All of a spider's legs are attached to the cephalothorax. This body part also contains the claws and feelers, the mouth and eyes, and the sucking stomach. At the back of the abdomen are three pairs of finger-like structures called spinnerets. Each of these contains as many as a hundred or more tiny spinning tubes. The silk that is made in special silk glands in the spider's abdomen is actually a liquid. It shoots out of the spinning tubes in fine streams and hardens into threads as soon as it hits the air. Some of the tubes produce a kind of liquid glue, which makes the silk strands sticky.

Spiders make several kinds of silk, each used for a different purpose. When a spider spins her web, she first lays out the spokes of the web, made of a heavy, dry silk. Then she goes around and around in a spiral, adding the elastic, sticky strands that will trap her prey. When a spider moves about in her web, she takes care to run along the dry strands. That is how a spider keeps from getting caught in her own web—she knows exactly where it is safe to step. Still another kind of silk is the fine "lifeline" that the spider spins out behind her wherever she goes. She can climb back along it quickly if necessary. Other types of spider silk are used to wrap up prey and to make round, cocoonlike cases for the spider's eggs, as she may carry her egg case around with her until her babies hatch.

Each kind of spider spins a different type of web. A young spider will spin a web of exactly the right pattern for her species, even if she has never seen any other spiders of her kind making webs. She seems to know just what to do. But scientists have found that certain drugs, such as LSD, will cause a spider to make mistakes. She may spin a crooked web or a web with parts missing.

Many kinds of spiders spin webs shaped roughly like a flat circle. This type of web may hang straight up and down or spread out horizontally, depending on the type of spider and where it lives. The webs of some spiders have their supports stretched out in all directions, such as the webs that house spiders spin in corners. Some spiders that live in the soil spin funnel-shaped webs, with the bottom of the funnel anchored in a hole or crack in the soil. The spider waits in the hole for prey to pass by. The trapdoor spider digs a hole in the soil and spins a tube-shaped silk lining for it. Then she builds a silk-lined trapdoor that covers the hole like a tight-fitting lid. When the trapdoor is closed, the outside of it looks exactly like a normal part of the soil and may even have plants growing on it. When

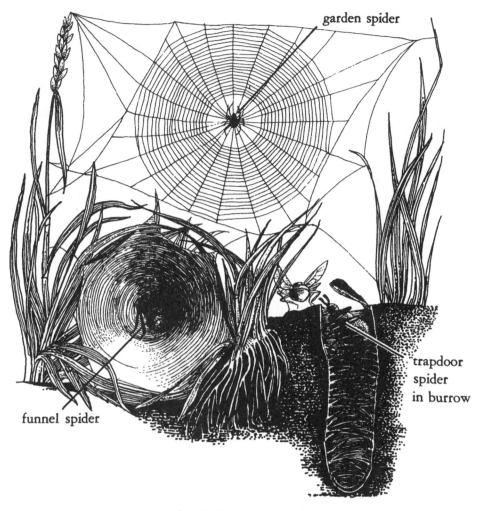

garden spider

trapdoor
spider
in burrow

funnel spider

Each kind of spider spins a different type of web.

the spider's prey, such as a pill bug or insect, passes by, the
trapdoor pops open on its silk hinge, and the trapdoor spider
swiftly snatches the unwary creature down into her burrow.

Some soil spiders do not spin webs at all; they use different
methods to catch their prey. One of these types lives under
stones or in the soil. It catches its prey by "spitting." Out of
clawlike structures in front of its mouth it can shoot sticky
threads. A researcher who took high-speed photographs of this
spider in action found that it can aim its "spittle" amazingly

accurately. Its prey is quickly covered with a tight zigzag of sticky thread from which even the slippery silverfish cannot escape.

The male spider is usually much smaller than the female. When he is ready to mate, he spins a small, simple web. On it he places a drop of liquid containing his sperms. Then he sucks the sperm liquid up into special compartments in the ends of his "feelers." Now he goes off to search for a female. He may woo her with touches or perhaps a special kind of courtship dance. When the female is ready, the male places his sperms inside her body. The courtship often has an unhappy ending for the male spider. The female may swiftly sting and eat him!

The female spider can store the eggs she has received from her mate for a long time—even more than a year in some cases. She mixes the sperms with her eggs, and she may have enough for several different batches of eggs. The mother spider spins a silken cocoon for her eggs, and within a few weeks dozens or even hundreds of young spiders hatch out. Some spiders care for their young and feed them for a time.

A spider's outer covering is a tough protective shell: a coat of armor. This shell cannot grow; the spider must shed its skin, or molt, in order to grow. It usually hides in a quiet crack when it is ready to molt. Its new skin is very pale and soft, and it could easily be attacked at this vulnerable time of its life. It also must remain as still as possible until its new shell has hardened, for if it moved around too much, its body might set into a crooked shape. A spider may molt as many as ten times before it is a full-grown adult. Most spiders live only about a year.

Although spiders are tiny, some of them have found a way to travel great distances. They sail through the air on silk balloons. On a fall day the air over a field may be filled with millions of spiders riding the winds on strands of silk. Each had climbed

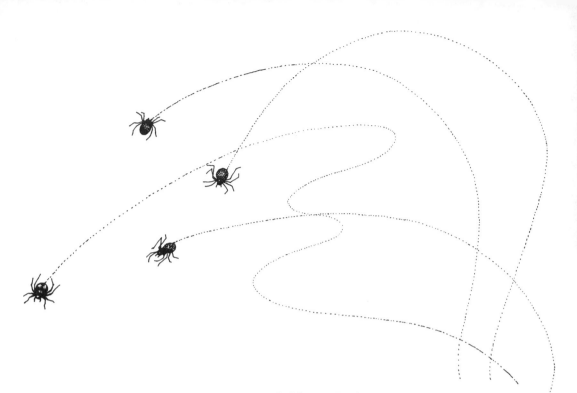

Spiders ride the winds on strands of silk.

up a plant stem and sent out silken threads that were caught by upward breezes.

Only a few spiders, such as the black widow spider, have venom strong enough to cause the death of a human. Among a group of the spiders' relatives, the scorpions, there are many kinds whose stings are very dangerous to humans.

Like spiders, scorpions have four pairs of walking legs. The pair of structures in back of a scorpion's mouth are usually very large and look like a lobster's claws. These claws are used for grasping the scorpion's prey. The scorpion's abdomen narrows down into a long, thin tail, with a powerful sting at the end.

Usually scorpions hide during the day, under rubbish or in small holes that they dig in the soil with their claws. They come out at night to hunt insects and spiders. They catch their prey with their claws and crush or tear it apart. The scorpion saves its sting as an emergency weapon, to be used only if its

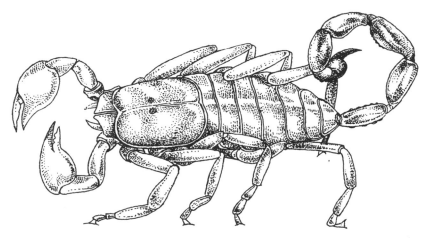

The scorpion is armed with claws and a sting.

prey puts up a violent fight or if some enemy threatens it. Then the scorpion curls its abdomen up over its body and jabs with its poison-filled tip. Curiously, small and medium-sized scorpions have the most dangerous stings. The large scorpions that live in the tropics and may grow to nearly a foot long can fight so well with their claws that they rarely need any other weapon. They use their stings mainly on other scorpions.

Scorpions mate in a manner very much like the springtails. During a courtship dance, the male places a droplet of sperms on a thin stalk attached to the soil. Then he leads the female into just the right position to pick it up. The young scorpions develop inside their mother's body. Scorpions do not lay eggs. Their babies are born alive. Usually the young scorpions ride about on their mother's back for many days before they go off to lead their own lives.

Another eight-legged relative of the spider is the harvestman, or daddy longlegs. Its legs are so long and thin that it looks as though it is walking on stilts. The legs are also very delicate and may break off if the daddy longlegs is handled roughly. However, missing legs will grow again the next time the animal molts.

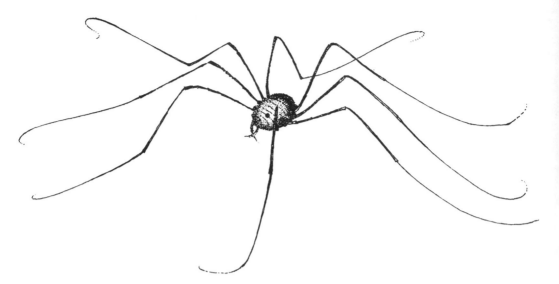

It is easy to see how the daddy longlegs got its name.

The daddy longlegs has only two eyes, and they are not very effective. It finds out about its world mainly by waving its sensitive second pair of legs about and touching everything in its path. This fragile-looking creature has no silk glands and no venom, but it is a hunter. It feeds on small insects, spiders, mites, and other harvestmen.

The long-legged harvestmen live in the layer of litter on top of the soil. They lay their eggs in cracks and under stones. Some short-legged forms live within the soil and feed on such soil-dwellers as small snails or springtails.

Spiders, scorpions, and harvestmen all belong to a group called arachnids, a name that comes from a Greek myth. Arachne, according to the story, was a girl from Lydia who was so proud of her skill as a weaver that she challenged the goddess Athena to a contest. The goddess was so angry at being challenged by a mortal that she changed Arachne into a spider.

Scientists also classify another important group among the arachnids: the mites and ticks.

Mites
TINY EIGHT-LEGGERS

SOME OF THE ANIMALS OF THE SOIL ARE LIFELONG INHABITANTS, remaining in the dark dampness of the underground world from birth to death. Others, like ants, snails, and some earthworms, may make their homes in the soil but come to the surface to feed or mate. Some soil creatures are only part-time inhabitants, spending a portion of their lives in the ground, then leaving it for a very different kind of home above the ground. Many butterflies, moths, and flies lay their eggs on or in the ground. The larvae, or young forms, may live and feed within the soil or crawl out to munch on plants. Then, when they are adults, they take to the air. Many creatures that live as parasites on plants and animals also spend part of their lives, as eggs or larvae, in the soil.

Mites and ticks, relatives of the spiders, include a fantastic variety of tiny animals whose lives fall into all these different patterns. People are most familiar with blood-sucking ticks and parasitic mites, such as chiggers. These annoying creatures are born in the soil. The young chiggers climb up the stalks of plants and wait. They cannot eat plants, and if no animal passes by within a few weeks, they will die. If an animal does brush against the plant, as many as a hundred chiggers immediately drop onto its skin. The parasites feed by piercing the skin of their victim and actually sticking their entire heads into it. A

69

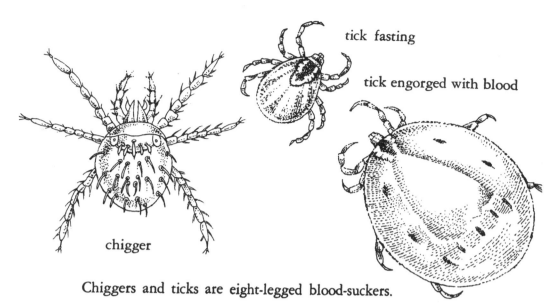

tick fasting

tick engorged with blood

chigger

Chiggers and ticks are eight-legged blood-suckers.

tick's head has a dartlike anchor that holds it so firmly in the skin that its head may snap off if the victim tries to brush it away. While they feed, ticks may transmit germs that cause diseases such as Lyme disease and Rocky Mountain spotted fever. Chiggers and other parasitic mites have a smoother anchor and are easier to brush off.

As soon as the chigger's head is anchored in its victim's skin, it injects a drop of chemicals that digests a narrow pathway into the skin. Body fluids soon come seeping out, just as water comes out of the ground when a well is dug. The chigger drinks in these fluids. After a few days, when it is full, it drops off unless the victim has managed to brush it off before this. Back on the ground the chigger grows to an adult, mates, and lays a batch of eggs.

Although ticks and chiggers are the best known to humans, most of the mites that live in the soil are not parasites at all. Some are predators, prowling through the soil or on its surface to attack insects and roundworms. Some feed on the eggs of plant lice and even other mites. Some eat plants or feed on bits of decaying matter.

70

The numbers of mites that swarm unseen beneath our feet can be fantastic. In your bucket of soil there may be more mites than all the other animals put together. They are found mainly in the top few inches of soil, where there is plenty of decaying matter and other soil animals to feed on.

How can it be that such vast hordes of mites swarm in the soil and most people have never seen them? Perhaps one reason is that mites are extremely tiny, as you might guess from their name. The largest are barely a quarter of an inch long.

If you found a young mite, you might think it was an insect, for it has only six legs. But later it will molt and grow eight legs like its spider relatives. Its body is quite different from both spiders and insects, for it is all in one piece, not divided into two or three parts. Some mites are pale and soft bodied, while others are covered with a coat of hard, dark-colored armor. These mites are called "beetle-mites," because they look a bit like miniature beetles. The armadillo mite, a member of this group, can fold the front part of its body against the hind part so that it looks like a tiny, round, hard ball. This ability helps to protect the armadillo mite from drying out. It is so effecive that the mite can live in much drier places than most soil animals and can even survive a few days of drought. Its coat of armor also helps to protect the armadillo mite from enemies, such as spiders and beetles.

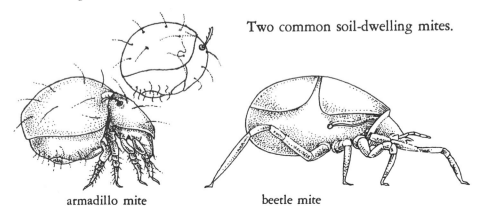

Two common soil-dwelling mites.

armadillo mite   beetle mite

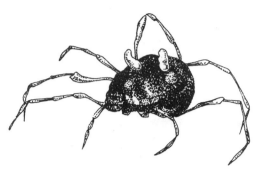

A horned beetle mite "nurse" carrying eggs attached to her body.

Although beetles are among the main enemies of the tiny mites, some kinds of mites spend part of their lives as parasites on beetles. Others cling as "stowaways" on the bodies of dung beetles when the large insects travel from one pile of decaying matter to another.

Just as mites vary enormously in their way of living, they also mate in quite varied ways, depending on their type. In some mites, the male has a special organ that places his sperms directly into the female's body. In others, the male places sperm droplets on stalks on the soil, much as the springtails do. The female, walking about, finds the droplets and picks them up. Most kinds of mites lay eggs in the soil or have special piercing needles to inject the eggs into the stems of plants. But some mites bear living young. The mother horned beetle mite attaches her eggs to the body of another female. This mite "nurse" carries the eggs about with her until they hatch. The eggs are so well protected in this way that the mother horned beetle mite lays only a few large eggs at a time instead of the dozens, or even hundreds, that are laid by animals that do not care for their young. In the dangerous jungle of the soil, where predators ceaselessly prowl the cracks and tunnels in search of food, survival for a species is usually gained in either one of two ways: by reproduction of enormous numbers or by special means of protection or defense.

Beetles
FLYING TANKS

THERE ARE MORE SPECIES OF BEETLES THAN OF ANY OTHER KIND of insects. Amazingly, more than 350 million different beetle species have already been discovered, and scientists believe there are many more that no one has studied yet. Indeed, new beetle species are reported each month.

Beetles can be found in just about every part of our earth where creatures can survive. Some live in the soil; others have taken to the water of ponds and streams. There are beetles that feed on plants, predator beetles that hunt insects and a variety of other animals, and scavenger beetles that feed on dead plants and animals and bits of decaying matter. Some beetles are almost too tiny to see; others, like the Hercules and Goliath beetles, are the largest of all the insects. Although most beetles are dull or dark colored, some species are as brightly colored as any bird.

Like many other insects, the beetle starts its life as a tiny egg, which soon hatches into a pale, wormlike grub (larva). It seems astonishing that the plump, soft grub will one day turn into a beetle with legs and wings and a hard, dark, shiny coat of armor.

The grub crawls about and seems to do nothing but eat. It gobbles down many times its own weight in plant leaves, insects, or whatever kind of food its species favors. You might expect that with all this eating, the grub would grow larger each day. But this is not the way insects grow. They are completely covered by a tough substance called chitin, which forms a jointed suit of armor. This chitin coat is a kind of outside skeleton, quite different from the inner skeleton of bones that we humans have. In addition to providing anchors for the muscles that help an insect to move, the chitin skeleton-on-the-outside also helps to protect it from drying out and gives some defense against its enemies. But this tough outer covering has some disadvantages, and one of these is that it cannot grow. Though the hungry beetle grub eats and eats, for a time it does not seem to be getting any bigger at all. It really is growing, but its new flesh is all wrinkled and squeezed inside its coat of armor.

At last the grub's coat is so tight it seems it must burst—and so it does. A new outer covering has formed beneath it. This skeleton is still soft, but is soon hardens into a much larger shape that gives the beetle grub more room in which to grow.

A variety of beetles inhabit the world of the soil.

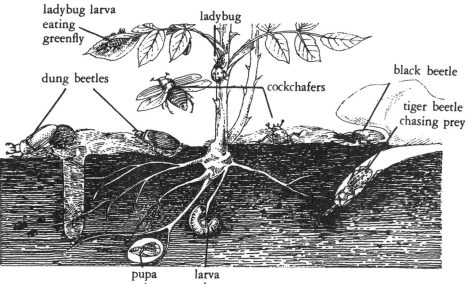

ladybug larva eating greenfly

ladybug

dung beetles

cockchafers

black beetle

tiger beetle chasing prey

pupa   larva
   cockchafer

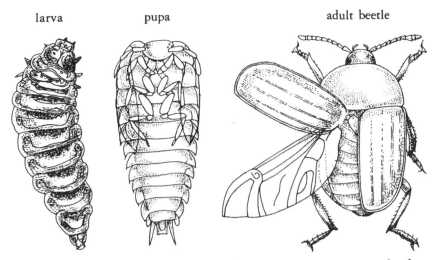

larva   pupa   adult beetle

The beetle's life cycle is made up of three separate stages: the larva, the pupa, and the adult.

The beetle grub will molt, or shed its outer skeleton, a number of times. Then chemical signals inside its body tell it that it is time to begin the amazing changes called metamorphosis. The larva settles down in some protected place, within a crack or under a stone, perhaps snuggled inside a special case it has built for itself. Now the insect is called a pupa. It looks like a tiny mummy, and indeed, it hardly seems alive at all. Inside its protective case, changes are taking place. Nearly its whole body seems to melt, and it turns into a liquid. From this "chemical soup," new structures are formed, and soon a pale image of a beetle begins to take shape. At last the pupa darkens, and an adult beetle breaks out of its case to begin a new kind of life.

Like all insects, beetles have six legs and a body that is divided into three parts, a head, a thorax, and an abdomen. A pair of eyes and a pair of "feelers," or antennae, mounted on top of its head, bring the beetle a picture of the world around it. Chewing mouthparts permit beetles to eat a great variety of solid foods, and many kinds of beetles live successfully even in places where liquids are scarce.

Like some other kinds of insects, most beetles have two pairs of wings. The two pairs are quite different. The front wings form a hard, tough shield that covers and protects the beetle's whole body. Neatly folded under this shield are the hind wings. These are the flying wings. The beetle can spread them wide quite quickly and take to the air to escape an enemy or search for food or a mate. The beetle is not a very graceful flier, nor can he fly very fast, but his wings seem to work well enough for his needs.

Among the most common beetles that live in the soil are the ground beetles. Many of them have shovel-like feet, which they use to dig burrows in the soil. Ground beetles are mainly hunters, feeding on insects, earthworms, snails, and other soil dwellers. Some of them have developed an unusual form of chemical warfare to protect themselves from their enemies. They send out a burning acid that is so strong it can blister your skin. The bombardier beetle is the champion at this kind of defense. If an ant or spider or even a larger enemy like a frog attacks a bombardier beetle, the insect mixes some chemicals in a special, hard-walled chamber inside its body. The chemicals react with each other and actually explode. Out comes a stinging mist of poison gas. The beetle can aim its weapon with amazing accuracy, and can fire again and again. An ant may suffer from fits for a long time after a dose from this "chemical cannon," and even a frog will back away, allowing the beetle to escape.

Another fierce hunter of the world of the soil is the tiger beetle. Most tiger beetles are dark colored or patterned to blend with the soil, but some have bright, jewel-like colors. The adults run about on the surface of the ground, searching for insects, particularly caterpillars. The larvae of the tiger beetle are also skillful hunters, using a very different technique. The

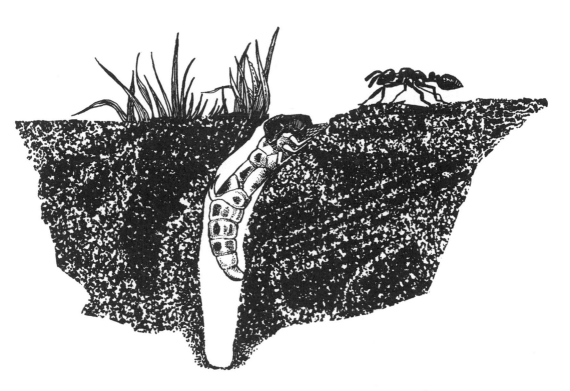

The tiger beetle larva lies in wait for its prey.

larva digs himself a short, tubelike burrow in the soil and lurks inside it. His head has a flat, brown top that exactly fits the opening of the burrow. He waits quietly, with his head bent over so that it neatly plugs the top of the burrow and blends with the soil. As soon as an insect or other creature passes nearby on the surface of the soil, the tiger beetle larva pops out like a jack-in-the-box and snatches his prey with his long, knifelike jaws. The prey may struggle and try to pull the larva out of his burrow, but two curved hooks on a hump on the larva's abdomen anchor him firmly. If there is danger or if the larva is not hungry, he can pull out his anchor and drop down to rest in the cool space at the bottom of the burrow.

Various scavenger beetles, such as carrion beetles and dung beetles, can be important in helping to enrich the soil. Carrion beetles feed mainly on dung (animal wastes), dead animals, and decaying plant matter. The burying beetles are carrion beetles that actually bury the bodies of dead animals in the soil. They dig away loose soil under the body, and it sinks deeper and deeper. Two or three beetles, working this way, can completely cover the body of a mouse within a few minutes. Safe under the soil, the beetles can feed on their prize without having to share it with maggots and various scavengers that roam the surface. The females lay their eggs in the carrion, and the larvae that hatch out have a ready source of food. They help to break down the bodies of dead animals and return their chemicals to the soil.

Dung beetles feed on piles of manure left by large animals on the surface of the soil. They bury this manure or dung in the soil, and since they usually eat only a small portion of the dung they gather, they help to provide food for other soil animals. The dor beetle, for example, comes out of the soil on warm nights and flies about, searching for dung. As soon as a dor beetle finds a pile of manure, it digs a tubelike shaft under it and quickly brings down pieces of dung to fill the shaft. During the day, or when the weather is bad, the dor beetle feeds on the dung it has gathered. But on the next warm night it flies off to seek a new dung pile, and it does not return to its old burrow again. In the fall, males and females mate and work together to dig a number of shafts, which they fill with

Dung beetles cooperate to dig shafts for eggs.

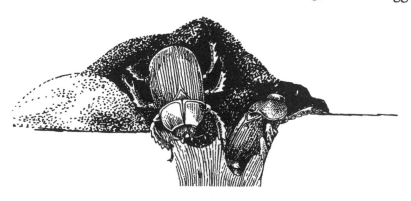

scarab

stag beetle

Beetles . . .

dung after the female has laid a single egg at the bottom of each shaft. The larvae feed and grow in their nursery tunnels and come out as adults the following summer.

A famous dung beetle is the scarab. This beetle was worshiped as a god by the ancient Egyptians, and its shape is still used in jewelry. Some scarabs have a curious habit of shaping fresh dung into a hard ball and rolling it away. The ball of dung may be many times larger than the beetle. He rolls it by turning his back to the ball and pushing with his hind legs while his front legs are braced firmly against the ground. Sometimes another scarab may come along and help the first beetle push his ball. The second scarab may try to steal the dung, but more often the two beetles bury the dung and themselves and share the food. Later, when it is the season for mating, scarab mates work together as a team to find and bury rich manure from which the female builds a pear-shaped nursery in which she lays an egg. The larva that hatches out is so well fed and protected inside its pear-shaped dung cell that its mother lays only a few eggs during the whole season.

Another useful scavenger beetle is the stag beetle. This forest dweller lives on rotting wood and helps to break down fallen logs and branches. It gets its name from the enormous jaws of the male, which look very much like the antlers of a male deer. Some scientists believe that the stag beetles use their enormous jaws when they fight for a mate. But they are so heavy and awkward that they are not very good for biting anything, even another stag beetle. The females have much shorter jaws, which are powerful enough to draw blood if they nip an unwary human handling them.

The scavenger beetles and the many beetle predators that feed on insects and other pests are very useful to man. But the group of beetles also includes many members that are serious pests themselves. A swarm of Japanese beetles can strip all the leaves and fruit from a tree within minutes. Potato bugs and various other plant-eating beetles also cause great crop damage. Leaf chafers can harm plants in two ways. Not only do the adults eat leaves, but the larvae develop in the soil and eat the

and more beetles. Some are friends and some are enemies of man.

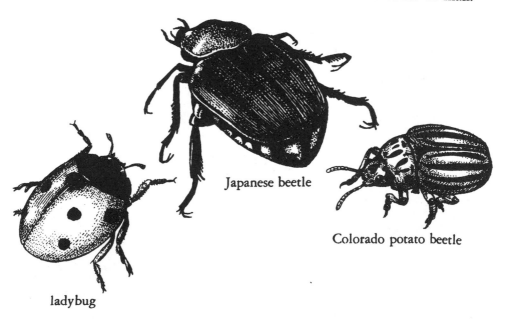

Japanese beetle

Colorado potato beetle

ladybug

roots of plants. These curled white grubs may take as long as three or four years to develop.

Controlling beetle and other insect pests is often a very difficult problem. Because the larvae develop in the soil, they are very hard to get at without killing *all* the animals of the soil, both good and bad. Chemical methods often backfire. For example, when farmers tried to get rid of cabbage-root flies by DDT treatments (later banned in the United States for most uses), they soon found that there was *more* damage instead of less. A study of the life of the cabbage-root fly revealed that there are more than thirty different kinds of beetle predators that eat cabbage-root-fly eggs, larvae, or pupae. The insecticide killed the "good" insects and scarcely harmed the pest at all. Now scientists are searching for biological methods of controlling pests. They study the life of the pest and try to find diseases and natural enemies that will kill it. They also search for ways to keep it from mating successfully, so that new generations of pests will not be born.

For example, Bt is a "natural insecticide" that now is used very widely. A bacterium *(Bacillus thuringiensis)* found in soils, it infects the larvae of many insect pests. A powder containing Bt spores (resting forms of the bacterium) can be applied to plant leaves. When insect larvae eat the leaves, they take in Bt, which begins to grow and develop inside their bodies. The bacterium makes a poison that kills the larvae quickly, before they can grow into adults and reproduce. Some kinds of Bt kill caterpillars. Other kinds work on beetle larvae, and one variety can kill mosquitoes and black flies. Researchers even have made plants such as corn resistant to insects by inserting genes from the bacterium (which contain the instructions for making the Bt poison) into the plants.

Ants
UNDERGROUND KINGDOMS

YOU PROBABLY HAVE A KINGDOM IN YOUR BACKYARD. HIDDEN from sight, in a spacious cavern under the ground, thousands of workers toil, cleaning and storing food and caring for the young in large "community nurseries." Soldiers fiercely defend the frontiers of the kingdom from foreign invaders. The kingdom is ruled not by a king, but by a queen. Courtiers surround her and care for her every need, for she is truly the queen mother of them all.

The kingdom of the ants is a dark place of branching tunnels and rooms, each painstakingly dug out, a grain at a time, by the ant workers. Some ant nests are built in mounds of dirt and twigs that the ants have built. Ant tunnels may go down as much as sixteen feet into the ground, and the largest nests can spread out beneath a whole acre of a field or pasture!

Ants have the typical insect shape, with six legs and a three-part body: head, thorax, and abdomen. The divisions between the parts of an ant's body are so sharp that it looks almost like three separate beads strung on a wire. Some ants, which spend their entire lives underground, are blind. But others have a pair of compound eyes, like those of most other insects. The eyes of an insect are quite different from ours. Each of our eyes contains a single lens, shaped like the lens of a camera or a telescope. This lens focuses the light rays that reach the eye and forms the image we see. The compound eye of an ant is a

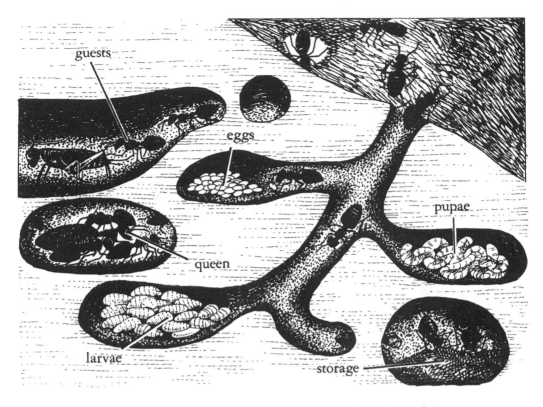

guests

eggs

pupae

queen

larvae

storage

The underground kingdom of the ants.

combination of many tiny lenses—dozens or even a thousand of them. Each tiny lens contributes a small part of the picture of the world. All these parts are put together in the ant's brain like the tiles of a mosaic to make the whole picture.

Even ants that have good eyes do not depend on them nearly as much as we depend on our eyes. Their sense of touch, especially in the two slender antennae at the top of the head, brings them much important information about their world. They also rely on their very fine sense of taste and smell. Indeed, ants constantly smell and lick each other whenever they meet. That is how they recognize members of their own colony. If they meet a strange ant from another colony, she will not have the right smell, and they will attack and kill her immediately. If, however, the intruder manages to sneak in

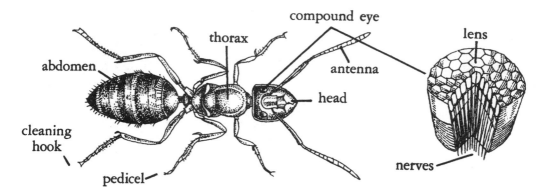

An ant. It clearly shows all the typical insect body parts.

unobserved, she will soon take on the smell of the nest, and the ants will leave her alone even though she does not look like them at all.

Some ant species make a practice of this kind of deception. A strange queen slips into an anthill and waits until her smell matches that of the nest. Then she goes boldly to the royal chamber, kills the rightful queen, and makes the workers her slaves! Other species of robber ants may dig narrow tunnels leading into the nest of a larger species. Whenever they are hungry, they raid the home of the larger ants and steal their food or even their larvae to eat. The larger ants cannot follow them into their narrow tunnels.

Even some creatures that are not ants may share the ants' home and food. A great variety of aphids, beetles, cockroaches, crickets, flies, and silverfish live as ant guests. Some of them make a sweet-tasting food that the ants lick from their bodies. The ants seem to love this food so much that they will care for their guests and even give them ant eggs and larvae to eat.

Ants are one of the groups of social insects. They live and work together and cooperate in the various tasks of the colony. Some are warriors, fierce fighters with knifelike jaws. They

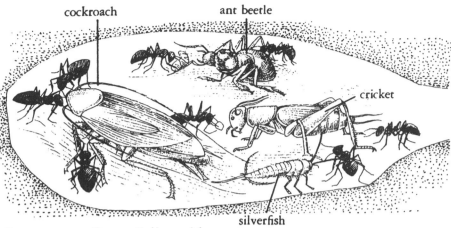

cockroach   ant beetle

cricket

silverfish

Some strange "guests" live with ants.

defend the nest from invaders or go out on raids into other ant nests. Some ants are workers. They build and clean the nest, gather and store away food, and care for the queen and the young ants. Amazingly, *all* the worker and warrior ants are females. Worker ants are probably the only ones you have ever seen. They are the ones who travel out of the nest, looking for food. If a worker ant finds a crumb of bread or some other bit of food, she may carry it back to the nest herself. Ants are quite strong, and they can carry loads many times their own size. If there is more food than the ant can carry, she will return to the nest and run about excitedly, poking other ants she meets and making noises by rubbing parts of her abdomen together. Some of the other workers will leave the nest and head for the food. They will find it even if the worker who first discovered the food does not go with them. For on her way back to the nest she carefully touched the tip of her abdomen to the ground from time to time, leaving an odor trail that her nestmates could follow.

Back in a large chamber in the nest, the queen of the colony works hard at her only job: laying eggs. Within her body she has a supply of sperms that she received from her mate on her marriage flight. She will keep these sperms for her whole life—

as long as fifteen or twenty years—and use them as she needs them. Before she lays each egg, the queen has a choice. She can mix some sperms with the egg. Then it will become fertilized, and the ant that grows from the egg will be a female. Or the queen may keep her bag of sperms tightly closed and lay an egg that will not be fertilized. This ant will be a male. Very few males are born, and these are drones. They do not do any work in the nest. Their only job will be to mate with the young queens.

Most of the ants in the colony are workers. But when the group is large and well established, some of the wormlike ant larvae develop into larger forms with wings. These are the young queens and drones. They stay around the nest for a few weeks. Then, on a hot summer day, they all take flight. This is the ants' marriage flight. Queens and drones fly in pairs and mate. The males will soon die, but the young queens go off to found new colonies—if they can escape the birds and other predators that are attracted to the swarm of flying ants.

The young ant queen digs herself a small chamber in the ground or in a rotting log and seals it off. There, quiet and protected, she sheds her wings and lays a batch of eggs. When the eggs hatch, the queen must care for them herself and feed them with food stored in her body. She grows tired and hungry, but soon her ordeal will be over. All the young ants are workers. They are smaller than normal, because the queen could not feed them very well while they were growing, but they quickly take up all the tasks of the group. They make the nest larger, gather food, and care for the queen and her new eggs. She will never have to do anything but lay eggs again.

Ants eat a variety of things, depending on their species. Many feed on the bodies of dead animals. Some are deadly hunters, who prey on springtails and other insects that live in the soil.

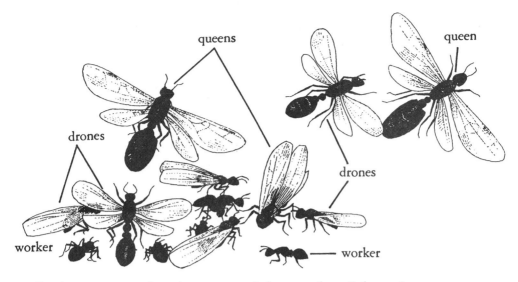

In the summer, winged queens and drones take off from the ant nest on a marriage flight.

Some ants gather the seeds of weeds and grasses and store them in underground granaries. If their stored seeds begin to sprout, the ants carry them outside and dump them near the entrance to the anthill. The seeds may then take root and grow into new plants. This practice has given some people the idea that these ants are planting gardens. But there is no reason to believe that the ants know what will happen when they take the seeds out or that they do it purposely.

Some ants do raise gardens underground. Leaf-cutter ants are found in various parts of the world. They come out of their nests and climb up trees and bushes to cut off leaves or parts of leaves. In single file the ants parade down again, each carrying a piece of leaf over her head like a parasol. They do not eat the leaves. Down in their underground caverns, worker ants chew the leaves into a soft mash, which they spread out onto flat beds. On the leaf mash they plant spores of a fungus. Their queen brought spores of this fungus with her from her marriage flight, tucked away in a special pouch in her mouth. The leaf-cutter ants tend their fungus garden carefully, fertilizing it

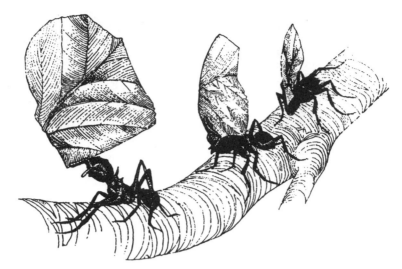

Leaf-cutter ants cut pieces of leaves and carry them like parasols.

with their droppings and pulling out stray weeds. It is the fungus that these ants eat.

Other ant farmers are "ranchers." They care for herds of aphids, plump little insects that live by sucking the juices of plants. Aphids make a sweet juice called honeydew, which ants love. The ant farmer comes up behind one of her aphid "cows" and gently strokes its abdomen. Out squirts a drop of honeydew, which the ant neatly catches in her mouth and swallows. The ant actually has two stomachs. The first one is called the "social stomach." The ant stores food in it temporarily and later shares it with the group. It is in the second stomach that the food for the ant's own needs is digested.

Many ants take good care of their aphid "cows." They may move the aphids from one plant to another and store their eggs in the nest over the winter. If the aphids are attacked, the ants will fight fiercely to defend them. Often the attackers are other ants—"cattle rustlers" of the insect world.

Scientists believe ants are among the most intelligent of all the insects. They can learn the way to food sources, and some can remember these routes even when the original odor trails

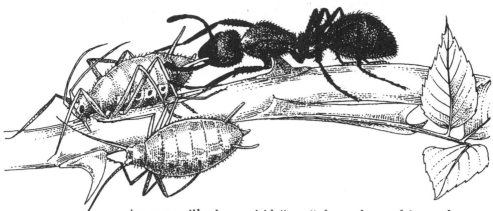

An ant milks her aphid "cow" for a drop of honeydew.

are gone. Ants can be taught to travel through rather complicated mazes, with as many as ten wrong choices. After a while the ant can go through the maze without making a mistake. But if the ant learned the maze while it was going from the anthill to food, and then the maze is turned around so that it is facing the anthill, the ant must learn the correct set of choices all over again. Ants can figure out ways to solve problems, such as getting over obstacles on the way to their food or nest. They are among the most interesting of all the soil creatures to study.

You can raise your own ant colony easily. If you see an ant on the ground carrying a bit of food, watch carefully to see where it goes (A bit of sugar bait will soon attract some ant scouts.) The ant will lead you to the entrance to its anthill. After you have found the hole in the ground that ants enter and leave, dig carefully in a wide circle around it. Gently scoop up as many ants as you can find, along with the pale grubs, pupae, and eggs. If you find an especially large ant among the others, this may be the queen.

A number of ready-made ant nests are sold in pet shops or toy stores. But you can make one by placing a small jar inside a larger, wide-mouthed jar. Fill the narrow space between the two jars with soil, and wrap heavy brown paper around the outside of the large jar. Place the ants, grubs, pupae, and eggs you have gathered on the soil, and cover the large jar with tight-fitting paper, with many tiny pinholes punched in it for air. Feed the ants every few days by placing some sugar and cooked meat or dead insects on top of the soil. Keep the soil moist, but not wet.

After the ants have had a week or so to get used to their new home, you can remove the paper and see the tunnels they have dug in the soil. With a magnifying glass, you can watch many details of ant life. You may see an ant cleaning herself or caring for the young. You might even catch an ant sleeping, with its legs tucked in close to its body, or stretching when it wakes up.

You can run many experiments with your ants. How do they handle large pieces of food, too large for one ant to carry? What will happen if you place a bit of food in the center of a bottlecap filled with water? Will the ants swim across to get it? If an ant is taken out of the jar, will it try to return to its new home, or will it try to run away? What will happen to a strange ant placed in the jar? Is there any way you can keep it from being attacked? These are only a few of the experiments you can try with ants. What others can you think of?

A simple ant cage you can make.

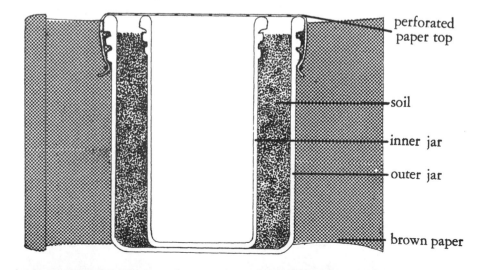

perforated paper top

soil

inner jar

outer jar

brown paper

Humans and the World of the Soil

EACH YEAR MORE OF THE EARTH'S SOIL IS COVERED WITH ASPHALT and concrete. New highways and buildings and airports are built. The soil beneath them is cut off from the life-giving oxygen of the air, and many of the soil creatures die. As people spread out into the countryside, forests and fields shrink; and the backyards and lawns that take their place are inhabited by very different creatures of the soil.

Every time a dam is built, hundreds, or even thousands, of acres become flooded, and most of the soil dwellers drown. When swamps are drained and their soil becomes dry, very few of the inhabitants can survive.

Even the farmer, while plowing up a field, can greatly change the soil communities. Fertilizers and pesticides used to help the crops grow better kill whole groups of soil dwellers but create better conditions for others to multiply.

Nearly every day we read about problems of pollution. Waste products from industry and automobile exhausts are poisoning our air and water. The detergents we use for dishes and clothes are washed into rivers, streams, and lakes. The plastic containers that foods and other items are packaged in litter the countryside and cannot be broken down by the soil organisms. Even the salt that is used to keep highways free of snow in the winter can kill trees and bushes by the roadside and can seep through

People's activities are changing the worlds of the soil.

the soil into our drinking-water supplies. Scientists do not yet know just how great the effects of all these pollutants are upon the world of the soil, but they surely must be important and growing more serious all the time.

We must learn, and learn quickly, more about how human activities are changing the world of the soil. For we depend on the soil for our very lives. The fruits and vegetables we eat grow in the soil. Meat animals graze on grass and eat fodder grown in soil. Soil animals help to free minerals and other nutrients from the remains of dead organisms to be used again

92

by the living. These substances pass from the soil into plants, and through foods into our bodies. Pesticides and pollutants can move along these same living chains.

Scientists are now beginning to study the communities of soil animals to learn more about how human activities are affecting the world of the soil and our own world. Comparisons of the populations of various species under different soil conditions can reveal the effects of pollutants and other poisons. Studies of animals such as springtails, mites, earthworms, and beetles may give us new insights into how harmful effects can be reduced and how the helpful creatures of the soil can be encouraged to grow and multiply.

Soil animals are being studied in laboratories all over the world.

Further Reading

Bourgeois, Paulette. *Amazing Dirt Book.* Reading, Massachusetts: Addison-Wesley, 1990.

De Bourgoing, Pascale. *Under the Ground.* New York: Scholastic, 1995.

Evans, Howard E. *Life on a Little-Known Planet.* Reprint edition. New York: Lyons Press, 1993.

Fowler, Allan. *Animals under the Ground.* Danbury, Connecticut: Children's Press (a division of Grolier), 1997.

Halfmann, Janet. *Life Under a Stone.* Jefferson, Louisiana: Creative Education, 2000.

Lavies, Bianca. *Compost Critters.* New York: Dutton, 1993.

Phinney, Margaret Yatsevitch. *Exploring Underground Habitats.* Greenvale, New York: Mondo Publ., 2000.

Ruffault, Charlotte. *Animals Underground.* Ossining, New York: Young Discovery Library, 1988.

Schwartz, David M. *Underfoot.* Huntington Beach, California: Creative Teaching Press, 1997.

Weber, Eldon. *Earthworm Empire: The Living Soil.* Dubuque, Iowa: Kendall/Hunt, 1996.

Index

Italics indicate illustrations